ARTIFICIAL INTELLIGENCE

ARTIFICIAL INTELLIGENCE

How Machine Learning Will
Shape the Next Decade

Matt Burgess

3 5 7 9 10 8 6 4 2

Random House Business
20 Vauxhall Bridge Road
London SW1V 2SA

Random House Business is part of the Penguin Random House
group of companies whose addresses can be found at
global.penguinrandomhouse.com.

Penguin
Random House
UK

First published by Random House Business in 2021

www.penguin.co.uk

A CIP catalogue record for this book is available from the British
Library.

ISBN 9781847943231

Typeset in 9.5/18 pt Exchange Text
by Integra Software Services Pvt. Ltd, Pondicherry

Printed and bound in Great Britain by Clays Ltd, Elcograf S.p.A.

The authorised representative in the EEA is Penguin Random House
Ireland, Morrison Chambers, 32 Nassau Street, Dublin D02 YH68.

Penguin Random House is committed to a sustainable future for
our business, our readers and our planet. This book is made from
Forest Stewardship Council® certified paper.

Contents

Introduction

The age of artificial intelligence has arrived. Since the turn of the millennium the nascent technology being developed in research labs for decades has crept into our everyday lives. It may not look like the sci-fi versions of AI fed to you through popular culture, but it is here. And it is making a huge difference to the world.

By the point in the day that you're sitting down to read this book or having it piped into your ears through an audio version, you will have interacted with AI multiple times. In almost every case, you may not have realised it was happening. It's now so ubiquitous in some of the products you use each day that you scarcely notice it.

Facebook posts you 'Liked' in your News Feed were shown to you because the company's AI has been monitoring your past activity and can forecast the ones you're most likely to give the thumbs-up. Netflix has been pushing films and shows at you because it already knows what you like. When you unlock your iPhone through facial recognition, this is because Apple's algorithms have mapped your features and matched them with your stored faceprint.

Every Google search you do surfaces AI-fuelled results, generated by scraping the entire web's contents and ranking what may be most relevant to your search. Maps on your car's satnav generate the fastest routes based on a real-time understanding of movement data and knowledge of the world. And every time you mutter 'Alexa' – or Amazon's smart speaker thinks it hears you say the wake-word – AI processes what you have said and delivers what it calculates to be the most appropriate response.

It's not just our everyday lives that are being transformed. In realms as diverse as healthcare and space exploration, AI is learning from reams of data collected over decades to help discover new drugs and hunt for new planets. Meanwhile, organisations from private companies to governments are increasingly using AI to improve their operations, reducing the administrative burden on people doing repetitive jobs.

And we're still in the fairly early days of the AI revolution. Over the next decade or so, there's huge potential for AI to overhaul many of our most everyday activities – think self-driving cars and robotic delivery – and bring further benefits to the world. The technology will come to lead the fight against credit card fraud, help detect images of child sexual abuse being uploaded to the internet, and identify cyberattacks before they cripple businesses.

As with all technologies, there are upsides and downsides to what AI has achieved so far and might in the future. On the upside, it is being democratised. Whereas AI used to be the preserve of companies with huge resources, now it's available to anyone who wants to go online and buy the tools to implement it. Ultimately both companies and individuals with no technical knowledge whatsoever will be able to make use of AI with ease. And, of course, it's becoming ever more sophisticated.

But there are potential problems, too. Currently, the majority of the interactions we have with AI systems are relatively inconsequential: they are regular, (sometimes) seamless, and ultimately forgettable. An unhelpful search result, or a few repeated attempts to unlock your phone, aren't the sort of moments to be remembered for more than a few seconds. However, this technology can also be used to snoop on us and to monitor our every activity. It contains the power to threaten our civil liberties, our freedom and our human rights – and to an extent is already being used for just these purposes. It's therefore no surprise that the world of policing should have become fascinated by it, or that governments are racing to become dominant in AI. It's a technology that raises major questions of power and control.

There are also questions of racism and sexism. At the moment AI is developed and controlled by a small group of people – mostly white males working for technology companies. Such lack of diversity has had and will continue to have serious repercussions for millions whose lives could be affected by AI's systems. Early deployments of it have shown that AI and various forms of social oppression have a tendency to go together.

Ultimately, AI can be a huge force for good – it has already changed the world in profound ways. But the next decade will be crucial in determining how far that change will go, and the extent to which it will ultimately be a benefit to society. This book not only explains how we've got to this point, but also explores where we're likely to go next.

1

The early years

Artificial intelligence as we understand it today was born during the summer of 1956, in a low-key summer getaway at Dartmouth College in New Hampshire on the east coast of the United States.

Over the course of two months a group of computer scientists, brought together by John McCarthy, Nathaniel Rochester, Claude Shannon and Marvin Minsky, and convinced that computers could behave more like people, discussed how to improve on what some of the earliest machines were capable of. 'An attempt will be made to find how to make machines use language, form abstractions and concepts, solve kinds of problems now reserved for humans, and improve themselves,' the four lead researchers had written in a paper the year before they met at Dartmouth.[1] Their timing seemed right. After all, around half a decade earlier the British mathematician and scientist Alan Turing had ignited the field with his idea that machines would eventually be able to learn by themselves. The scientists' hope was that their summer of research would result in 'a significant advance' for machines.

In the event, the researchers were to be disappointed with their efforts. The workshop failed to get all the funding it needed; those invited could not agree on any common standards; and follow-up work was hampered by the participants having their own research to pursue. In any case, given the comparatively basic state of computers of the time, the Dartmouth summer project's goals were unrealistic. 'My hope for a breakthrough towards human-level AI was not realised at Dartmouth,' McCarthy wrote in a note fifty years later.[2]

But the workshop had an impact nevertheless. Before it took place, nascent artificial intelligence research had often fallen under the category of Automata Studies, which could lead to a somewhat disjointed approach. In the four researchers' original proposal, however, they had for the first time used the phrase 'artificial intelligence'. 'The term was chosen to nail the flag to the mast,' wrote McCarthy half a century later. The strategy worked. This new label kick-started what has now become a multi-billion-dollar industry, and McCarthy himself has been credited with its birth.

One key early development was the adoption of an old idea that would – after then dropping out of fashion again – come to define the modern age of artificial intelligence: neural networks. In the early 1940s, scientists had created the first mathematical models of neurons – the building blocks of the brain, which use electrical impulses and chemical signals to carry signals across the brain and throughout the body's nervous system – and set up electrical circuits to mimic them. In 1958, in the wake of the Dartmouth College meeting, and with funding from the US Office of Naval Research, the American psychologist Frank Rosenblatt built the first trainable artificial neural network. Dubbed Perceptron, and operating inside a room-sized machine of the same name, it involved an algorithm that could learn to recognise patterns and shapes presented to it.

Today's neural networks are much faster and more sophisticated than Perceptron, and each will be tailored differently to undertake a particular task, but many of the basic underlying principles remain much the same. Essentially, neural networks are a way of doing machine learning, whereby a computer learns by being exposed to previous examples of the task it's trying to complete, and thus eventually receiving all the information needed to replicate that task. For example, a neural network that's being developed to recognise pushbikes in photographs will be taught what pushbikes look like by being shown hundreds, even thousands, of images of pushbikes, each of which is labelled to say it's a pushbike. (Obviously when a machine 'sees' an image, it is not viewing it in the same way we would: what it sees is strings of numbers into which the photo and accompanying text have been broken down.) If the training process is successful the algorithm will then be able to identify bikes in photos it has not 'seen' before. Generally the more examples it is trained with (which of course adds more time and cost to the process), the more accurate its results. Following the same principle, other neural networks analyse vast quantities of numerical data in order to create new images, make predictions, translate languages, control self-driving vehicles and discover new drugs. Neural networks have found planets. They've made music and art. And all this is just the tip of the iceberg.

These systems are loosely modelled on the structure of the brain, with interconnecting neural nets comprising data-processing nodes in their thousands or millions, serving the same function as neurons. The Perceptron machine used only one layer of nodes, but modern systems can have multiple layers – in some cases up to fifty – that pass data through them. In neural networks with multiple layers, each of these layers has its own capabilities and can be trained to recognise different features. Such systems are now commonly called deep neural networks, and it's these that have contributed to many of the artificial intelligence developments achieved over the last two decades.

Broadly speaking, there are three types of layers in neural networks: an input layer, hidden layers and an output layer. The input layer is where information is fed into the neural network. The hidden layers do all the computer-processing (complex neural networks will have a large number of these). The output layer yields the final result. Nodes within each layer are connected to one another – there may be billions of connections in a large neural net system – and are all given numbers, known as weightings. (The weightings control how strong the connections between two nodes are, and so have an impact on the output.) Weightings are altered throughout the training process so that the final outputs are consistent and produce the results the creators of the system desire.

Rosenblatt's neural network could complete some very basic tasks, but because it used only one layer of nodes and a relatively simplistic weighting system its capabilities were severely limited. That's not how people at the time saw the Perceptron, though. At the end of July 1958, when the *New York Times* reported that the Perceptron could differentiate between left and right after just fifty training attempts, it went on to claim that the 'embryo' of a computer could one day be expected to 'walk, talk, see, write, reproduce itself and be conscious of its existence'.[3] It also reported Rosenblatt as saying that Perceptron could be 'fired to the planets' as part of future space exploration missions. He wouldn't be the last AI researcher to make bold claims, though it's worth noting that another early neural network called MADALINE, which was developed in 1959, was able to detect patterns in data and at least of rather more immediate and practical use than Perceptron: put to work eliminating echoes on phone lines being used for long-distance phone calls, it proved so effective that it was used for decades.[4]

The technical limitations of the first neural networks were laid bare in 1969, when the AI pioneer Marvin Minsky and mathematician Seymour Papert shot down the Perceptron algorithm in a book of the same title. This simplistic neural network, with just the one layer, they argued, wasn't capable of executing anything more than basic tasks – a far cry from the promised ability to be aware of its own existence.

Minsky and Papert's book has been widely credited with dampening the enthusiasm for neural networks. Certainly, after its publication research in the field dwindled. But overall, the 1960s saw a blossoming in AI research, and the creation of many of the key ideas that underpin current AI. US technology universities, including the Massachusetts Institute of Technology, Carnegie Mellon and Stanford, started researching the field, and were joined by leading technology companies. Funding was provided by the US military, including the Defense Advanced Research Projects Agency (DARPA). At the same time, the release of Stanley Kubrick's *2001: A Space Odyssey* and the soothing tones of the all-knowing and seemingly helpful HAL 9000 increased public awareness of AI, and planted the idea of a world where machines co-exist with humans. In 1972 such a future seemed to come a little closer with the development by the Stanford Research Institute International of a robot called Shakey. Essentially a cuboid-shaped computer on wheels, Shakey was able to identify objects on its own, navigate around them and then explain why it did so. Its movements may have been jerky (hence its name), and often nonsensical, but at the time it was cutting-edge.

By the early 1980s, researchers were creating set-ups – called expert systems – that could mimic the decision-making process of a human expert. They could, that is, provided that the tasks involved were very narrow and specific. Some of these systems achieved practical use. American Express, for example, used an expert system to help its staff determine whether people were exceeding credit limits on their cards.[5] IBM deployed the technology to help consultants work out how much after-sales services should be sold for. Other countries became intrigued. Japan invested huge sums in AI systems, which ultimately failed to produce significant results. It was a sign of things to come.

Overall, though, the 1970s and the late 1980s were lean times for machine learning. Indeed, they became known as the AI winters (named after the concept of nuclear winters). Lacking major breakthroughs, and employing technical systems that had reached their limits, the technology waned and research funding was duly cut. There was a general sense of disenchantment: AI had failed to meet the grand promises those working in the field had proposed. 'Most workers in AI research and in related fields confess to a pronounced feeling of disappointment in what has been achieved in the past twenty-five years,' said a 1973 report into the impact of AI commissioned by the UK's Science Research Council.[6] Those who had entered the field in the 1950s and 1960s had had 'high hopes' for the technology, but these were 'very far from having been realised'. 'In no part of the field', the report went on, 'have the discoveries made so far produced the major impact that was then promised.' The report's author, James Lighthill, singled out machine translation for particular criticism. It had the most 'notorious disappointments', he wrote: 'enormous sums have been spent with very little useful result.'

Around the same time the Lighthill report was published, DARPA, which up until then had been enthusiastically backing AI research, had a change of heart and eventually cut funding from some AI work. Some AI researchers were uneasy. They believed unrealistic expectations had been set for what the technology would be able to achieve, and that these had spread to those outside the industry. 'During the early 1980s, many AI sponsors, in government and in industry, had greatly inflated expectations of what AI could do,' wrote Nils Nilsson, an AI pioneer, in his 2009 book charting 50 years of the industry.[7] 'Undoubtedly, some of the blame for their unjustified optimism could be placed on AI researchers themselves,' he continued, 'who were motivated to make exaggerated promises.' As a consequence, he pointed out, the membership of an AI trade body fell, advertising in the industry's *AI Magazine* dropped, some AI companies closed and research at some of the biggest hardware and software companies came to a halt.

But then on 11 May 1997 came remarkable news. IBM's Deep Blue computer had beaten the chess grand master and former world champion Garry Kasparov by 3½ games to 2½. Kasparov had previously bragged that he would never lose to a machine, and had indeed beaten Deep Blue the year before. But this time he was stunned by its play. 'I'm a human being. When I see something that is well beyond my understanding, I'm afraid,' Kasparov said after he conceded the final game in the series.[8] A subsequent cover of *Inside Chess* magazine read: 'ARMAGEDDON'.

Deep Blue's victory over Kasparov marked a significant moment in the development of AI. It catapulted the technology and its capabilities back into the public domain. And since then AI has advanced almost exponentially, helped by increasingly powerful and lower-cost technology, and further fuelled in the past decade by cloud computing, improved hardware and smart new algorithms. Neural networks have become deep neural networks, and deep learning has flourished. Today a world without it seems unthinkable.

What is intelligence?

The driving force behind artificial intelligence has always been the desire to mimic and improve upon human capabilities. Ever since the phrase was coined in Dartmouth during the 1950s, the quest has been on to produce a machine that thinks like humans. The loftiest goals of all are to create a system of artificial general intelligence (more popularly referred to as AGI).

Depending on who you ask, AGI may be a system that's as smart as a human, or one that's even smarter, and able to complete any task asked of it. There is significant debate within AI research communities about what AGI might look like and, perhaps even more importantly, whether it is actually achievable.

At the moment, barring a sudden huge AI break-through, we're a long way from an all-knowing system that's able to answer any question, serve humanity's every need, or even take over the world. But arguably, too, we're still a long way from artificial intelligence that possesses even basic intelligence, as we understand it. And that raises the question of what intelligence actually is.

The short answer is that there's little agreement on the subject. When it comes to defining intelligence, experts within and across multiple disciplines, from neuroscience and psychology to philosophy, often disagree fiercely. When it comes to measuring intelligence, no current system wins universal approval (IQ tests, for example, are regarded by many as both limited and problematic). And when it comes to applying principles of intelligence to machine learning, interpretations vary. 'I don't think there's any real consensus definition of what the intelligence in artificial intelligence means,' says Henry Shevlin, a research associate at the University of Cambridge's Leverhulme Centre for the Future of Intelligence.

The concept of intelligence is further complicated by the fact that at various times in human history it has been weaponised to oppress and harm people. Between the eighteenth and twentieth centuries, some scientists claimed that inequality in the world was caused by biological differences in intelligence between races. Being intelligent was seen as the domain of white Westerners, who used it to drive colonialism and as a foundation for racism. Race science has declined since the Second World War but, as Angela Saini points out in her book *The Return of Race Science*, it is still endorsed by some, largely right-wing, groups.

In the sphere of AI, the erroneous notion of intelligence being white persists, according to Kanta Dihal, a researcher at the Leverhulme Centre for the Future of Intelligence. Dihal is working on two projects concerned with our understanding of AI: the first is about the narratives people use when referring to AI; the second (in collaboration with the centre's executive director, Stephen Cave) looks at decolonising AI. 'The whole concept of intelligence is usually taken for granted in the phrase "artificial intelligence",' says Dihal, 'but what is actually meant by the term "intelligence" is extremely political and extremely context-dependent.' The peak of intelligence in computer science traditionally involved a machine being good at chess. But as Dihal explains: 'That goes back to the late nineteenth and early twentieth century, when measures of intelligence were being instituted in order to establish and maintain hierarchies among humans.'

Defining intelligence within AI precisely, then, is fraught with problems and caveats. That said, a useful starting point is the often-used definition arrived at by researchers Shane Legg and Marcus Hutter (both are now based at the Google-owned AI company DeepMind, of which Legg is a co-founder). 'Intelligence', they suggested in 2007, 'is an agent's ability to achieve goals or succeed in a wide range of environments'[9] (the two men later refined their work into a mathematical equation for machine intelligence[10]). That 'agent' could be a human, an animal or a machine. So far as the 'goals' are concerned, these are considered to involve problem-solving, reasoning, and processing information quickly. All are common human traits, hence the reason why our understanding of intelligence is fundamentally based in ourselves.

In terms of machines, such capabilities at the moment tend to be restricted to narrow, rather than general, intelligence. Humans are able to learn from a wide set of experiences and apply what they've learned to new scenarios. AI can perform tasks at the level of humans, or in some cases above, if it's given enough examples. It is, however, specific and narrow. The Deep Blue system that beat Kasparov was one of the best chess players of all time, but it couldn't do anything else other than play chess. It couldn't even win at other games, let alone perform other, more general tasks. Even today, the AI we have isn't sophisticated enough to do more than one thing. To that extent, young children and animals can be considered to have more intelligence or capabilities than our best AIs.

Take the handling of objects, for example. 'You can't get robots to consistently manipulate objects in the way that a two-year-old or a three-year-old can interact with the world,' says Chelsea Finn, an assistant professor working on robotics at Stanford University. 'It seems like maybe we're missing some pretty fundamental things about intelligence.' Finn's work is partly focused on making robots replicate what humans can do, so they can be useful in the real world – the more general a robot's abilities, the more likely it can be used for different tasks. For this to happen robots have to understand how objects work in three dimensions, how an item can be handled, and what the consequences of moving an object around are. 'I think that if we are able to allow robots to have the skills to interface with the physical world,' says Finn, 'then there's a lot of things that they can do to help society, whether it be helping with disaster-relief situations, helping with things that deal with an ageing population, for example. It's a really hard problem in comparison to other applications,' she adds.

If general human abilities are a mark of intelligence, then, AI has a long way to go. And if we use the model of human intelligence to understand and depict intelligence in machines, this can distort the way we view AI technology. In Western culture, dystopian views of AI have focused on its inhumanity, from HAL, in *2001: A Space Odyssey*, to Ava in *Ex Machina*, to all the robots in *I, Robot*. Dihal points out that Russians generally expected early text chatbots to be as emotionally stunted as Arnold Schwarzenegger's Terminator character.

'In Japan, we have a more positive, utopian view,' says Toshie Takahashi, a professor studying the impact of AI at Waseda University, Tokyo. One narrative popular there involves Doraemon, a blue robot cat with neither claws nor ears that travels back in time to help a boy called Nobita Nobi. Perhaps the results of Takahashi's research suggest a future path for our relationship with AI. She has shown that almost 70 per cent of young people in the country have a positive image of it ('People talk more about social good or social benefits, especially for an ageing society'), but that 60 per cent of them don't want AI to be in humanoid form. In general, as Dihal points out, there's a gradual move to presenting AI as something that isn't human or a danger to society. 'There's an increase in exploring narratives where the artificial intelligence doesn't look exactly humanoid or isn't embodied at all.' In other words, we may be heading for a future where we don't judge AI in terms of human capabilities.

2

AI takes off

Jeff Dean and Andrew Ng didn't set out to teach their AI what a cat looked like – it learned on its own. 'It basically invented the concept of a cat,' Dean told the *New York Times* in 2012,[11] as the ground-breaking deep-learning research was published.

Dean and Ng's achievement, at Google's experimental technology lab X, showed just how far AI had come in the fifteen years since IBM's Deep Blue beat Garry Kasparov. That event had helped stimulate a resurgence of interest and research into AI. Over the following few years, AI would compete against humans at backgammon. The first robotic surgical systems were developed. Advances were made in machines' ability to recognise speech, understand written language and recognise hand-written digits.

Various factors made Dean and Ng's feat possible. By the start of the new millennium, the cost of hardware had dropped massively from just a decade before. It was much faster, too. In addition, AI researchers were benefiting from the discovery that the best computer chips to use for their work were not traditional central processing units (CPUs) but the graphics processing units (GPUs) that render the graphics in computer games (invented by Nvidia in 1999, they have around 200 times more processors per chip and can crunch data at faster speeds). Finally, with the global internet acquiring its first billion users by 2005 and the looming spread of smartphones, the amount of data available to 'train' neural networks was growing exponentially.

Given these advances, it was no surprise that AI was breaking out from niche computer science departments to Silicon Valley. Big tech's largest companies were now busy snapping up AI researchers, and paying them huge salaries to turn their attention to the vast datasets owned by their new employers. Google's lab X was a leading example.

To get their AI to learn what a cat was, Dean and Ng's team produced a giant network of 16,000 computer processors, with one billion connections, trained on ten million random YouTube video thumbnails.[12] The researchers hadn't primed the system with any prior data that contained labels for the objects shown. But gradually, as they were exposed to millions of similar pictures, individual neurons started to group objects in the YouTube thumbnails according to their characteristics. By the end of three days of training, the deep learning system could group cats with 74.8 per cent accuracy, human faces with 81.7 per cent accuracy and human body parts with 76.7 per cent accuracy. In total it could group objects across 20,000 different categories, involving improvements of 70 per cent on some previous image-recognition systems. The machine had taught itself to recognise objects – even if it didn't have any awareness of what they actually were. It's what unsupervised learning does particularly well: grouping similar objects in massive unorganised datasets in a way that helps researchers spot patterns they would otherwise have missed.

Another – arguably more significant – achievement in 2012 was made by the artificial neural network, later named AlexNet, created by three researchers at the University of Toronto: Alex Krizhevsky, Ilya Sutskever and Geoffrey Hinton – the latter a pioneer in the world of AI. Using a traditional convolutional neural network with a GPU for the first time, it achieved overnight fame by winning that year's ImageNet competition.[13] The competition was set up in 2010 and involved computer scientists vying against each other to build a system that could correctly categorise images contained in a free database of millions of hand-labelled images, from cars to bananas to children, in thousands of categories. Each image in the database has a description added by a human, and the competition was to see which AI system could most accurately identify images it had never seen before. AlexNet outperformed its competitors by more than 10 per cent, and because it used GPUs was able to process the millions of ImageNet images shown to it in around five or six days, as compared with the weeks or months it was taking for AI systems that used CPUs. This greater speed also allowed the Canada-based team to refine their results more frequently.

By 2015 further advances had been made in speed and accuracy. The winners of that year's ImageNet hit 96 per cent accuracy levels, besting human efforts at recognising objects in images for the first time. One year earlier, Facebook's person recognition DeepFace neural network hit accuracy levels of 97.35 per cent for some faces – just a quarter of a per cent lower than humans scored in the same test. Facebook's neural network was trained using 4.4 million labelled face pictures from 4,030 people using the social network.

It was at this time that another major player in the AI race started to garner headlines. DeepMind, a London-based AI company which Google purchased for a reported $400 million in 2014, had been a relatively obscure start-up. But it took the research world by storm with its announcement that its deep Q-network – a deep neural network using reinforcement learning – was able to win 49 classic Atari games, including *Space Invaders* and *Breakout*, despite being given only given limited information about them. 'We're trying to build a single set of generic algorithms, like the human brain,' the company's co-founder Demis Hassabis told *WIRED*.[14]

In March 2016 DeepMind took a quantum leap forward and, employing its AlphaGo system, managed to defeat the world champion of the 3,000-year-old board game Go. At one level, this might sound like an achievement on a par with Deep Blue's defeat of Kasparov a couple of decades earlier. But Kasparov had been able to go toe-to-toe with Deep Blue, drawing most of the matches in the series before resigning, head in hands, in the final game. And he had been playing chess. Go, which is played on a 19×19 board with white and black tokens, is infinitely more complex (many AI researchers didn't believe a machine would be able to beat the world's best human players for several decades), and Lee Sedol, the world's number-one

Go player, who had won the game's top title eighteen times, was, unlike Kasparov, trounced. He lost 4–1.

AlphaGo initially learned how to play by watching humans, but over time it developed its own decision-making skills. Under the hood were multiple neural networks, embodying years of AI progress, and the power of Google's global data centres. One neural network would select the next move to play. Another would aim to predict the winner of the game based on the moves so far made. The result was a system that didn't just regurgitate styles of play it had learned from watching thousands of human moves, but invented its own. In one particular match the machine directed the person laying the physical pieces to make a move so unexpected that no human would have thought to have made it. 'It's not a human move. I've never seen a human play this move,' said Fan Hui, a three-time European Go champion, who was commentating on the game and had worked with DeepMind to play hundreds of training matches against AlphaGo preceding its victory over Lee. 'So beautiful.'[15] It was almost creative.

Since that match against Lee the AlphaGo system has advanced further. In fact, it has gone beyond human knowledge. One version, dubbed AlphaGo Zero, learned how to play the game from scratch without being trained on previous human games – and in the process it learned to beat AlphaGo. DeepMind says it 'accumulated thousands of years of human knowledge' in just a few days. The next version, AlphaZero, was able to play not only Go but also chess and Shogi, without having to be adapted to play each different game.

On 30 November 2020, DeepMind announced that its AI systems had moved beyond games to crack one of biology's toughest challenges. Its AlphaFold system, it revealed, had managed to generate accurate 3D models of proteins, highly complex substances that are present in all living organisms.[16] Because proteins are large molecules that can 'fold' in a huge variety of ways before they assume their final form, they are notoriously difficult to model and predict. This breakthrough is highly significant, and, while it's still early days, offers the promise of ultimately giving us a much greater understanding of biological processes and of genes that cause diseases in humans. 'I do think it's the most significant thing we've done, in terms of real-world impact,' Hassabis said as AlphaFold's results were announced.[17]

Such extraordinarily rapid progress gives an indication of some of AI's potential. At present, it can master individual tasks quickly and efficiently. But researchers envision a future world where a single system can complete multiple tasks without needing to be adapted for each one. If that general-purpose vision is realised it will fundamentally alter how humans interact with machines – far more than it already has. As it happens, Lee's single win during his defeat by AlphaGo is the only time a human has ever been able to beat the system. But the overall loss had a profound experience on one of the greatest ever players of the game. He retired from it in 2019, sensing it would never be the same for him again. 'Even if I become the number one,' he said, 'there is an entity that cannot be defeated.'[18]

ARTIFICIAL INTELLIGENCE

Better tools, greater power

Such is the speed with which AI has spread – and continues to do so – that many of the innovations that only a few years ago were the preserve of a few labs and well-heeled Silicon Valley companies are now within the reach of most of us. The price of computers has continued to come down, and their power has increased. You can now buy a high-powered laptop or desktop that can run AI applications using Google's, Amazon's or Microsoft's cloud services, and you can train yourself how to use them. All you need is a decent internet connection and a few clicks of the mouse.

At the same time, further advances are being made in the hardware that drives AI. So, for example, while GPUs remain the preferred type of processor for running some AI applications, Google, Intel, Graphcore and a host of other start-ups are racing to build faster and more powerful AI chips. Google announced its Tensor Processing Unit (TPU) AI chip in 2016. Meanwhile, Graphcore, founded by Nigel Toon and Simon Knowles, has raised more than $400 million in venture capital funding to produce its Intelligence Processing Unit (IPU) chip. 'When Google announced they were building the TPU that was a big moment,' says Toon, Graphcore's CEO. 'It was the TPU that actually made people wake up and say, you actually need to build dedicated hardware for this.'

Graphcore's IPU was designed from scratch over half a decade not just to work specifically with the intelligent machines that are around today, but to anticipate further scaling of AI. The second version – which Toon says was the one it always intended to make – uses 59.4 billion transistors (electrical gates that switch on and off to perform calculations) that are packed just seven nanometres apart. The company says its Mark 2 chip can deliver eight times better performance compared to its first. The chips are interconnected so that they can communicate effectively with one another in a world where more data than ever will be thrown at increasingly complex AI systems. 'We know that these knowledge models we're going to build are going to actually end up being incredibly complicated,' Toon says. 'What we're trying to do is to create a piece of hardware that is rather more complex in terms of how it operates, so that you can actually exploit that fundamental sparsity that is there in the data.' The IPU is now in commercial operation.

Big data – the lifeblood of the AI revolution – is improving, too, in terms of its quality and sheer quantity. 'People started to recognise that the way to advance was not just to have clever algorithms and lots of compute power, but what you needed is training data, that has been very carefully curated,' says Michael Wooldridge, a professor of computer science at the University of Oxford and the programme co-director for AI at the Alan Turing Institute. Satellites around the world are now capturing the planet in high resolution, a version of the world's history has been freely documented on Wikipedia, our cities are increasingly full of sensors that can track everything from footfall in streets to how full bins are. At a personal level: each tap on your smartphone creates a data point, watching habits are stored, medical records are going digital and people are uploading more images and video to the web.

In the wrong hands, of course, such data can endanger privacy and enable abuse. But in the right hands it can be used to train machine-learning systems in ways that lead to active improvements in the world around us. Researchers are using big data to program drones that can survey deforestation and replant seeds. Big data has helped AI to discover new antibiotics from hundreds of millions of molecules. NASA data has been crunched to find new planets. The list goes on.

It's not just AI tools that are on the rise. The sector itself is getting bigger and attracting ever more investment. According to data collected by the AI Index, a project run by Stanford University to analyse the global state of the industry and how it is changing, AI start-ups raised $1.3 billion in 2010. In 2018 the figure hit $40.4 billion. And while 2020's global pandemic may have led to a temporary downturn, the overall direction of travel is still upwards. More than 3,000 AI companies received funding in 2018. Between 2014 and November 2019 more than 15,000 investments of more than $400,000 were made in AI companies – the average size of investment being approximately $8.6 million. In the process, thousands of additional staff have been taken on by the big technology companies. AI research divisions have been boosted. And new players have been drawn in outside the magic circle of deep-pocketed tech companies – from pharmaceutical companies to banks.

AI is also now a global enterprise. Investment may still be largely dominated by the US and China, who are battling to become AI superpowers, but other regions of the world are also spending big. 'Whoever becomes the leader in this sphere will become the ruler of the world,' said the Russian president Vladimir Putin in 2017.[19] When adjusted to reflect population levels, investment in 2018 and 2019 showed countries as diverse as Israel, Singapore and Iceland to be drivers in AI innovation. 'One thing is certain,' says the 2019 AI Index report: 'whether directly or indirectly, AI systems play a key role across businesses and shape the global economy for the foreseeable future.'[20]

There's been a corresponding explosion in AI publications and conferences. The AI Index has shown that in the 20 years between 1998 and 2018 there was a 300 per cent increase in the number of peer-reviewed AI scientific papers. Today China publishes as many AI journal and conference papers a year as the whole of Europe, having surpassed the US as the single biggest contributor. And the biggest AI research conference, NeurIPS, had 13,000 attendees in 2019, up 800 per cent compared to 2012.

Today the AI field has multiple sub-domains, from pattern-matching to voice recognition, via computer vision, which teaches machines to 'see', and natural language processing, which allows machines to understand text. And yet arguably we're still early on in the commercialisation of a technology that is already so ubiquitous in some areas. Even now, understanding where and what type of AI is being used can be a challenge – one analysis in 2019 judged that 40 per cent of AI start-ups in Europe don't actually use AI.[21] And although we've seen rapid expansion over the past decade, it's taking a while for the world as a whole to catch up. Oxford's Michael Wooldridge argues that AI's practical use is still at a relatively early stage. He likens its growth to that of the Web, which, though invented in 1989, didn't really make it into people's workflows until around fifteen years later (and even today many industries still rely on the printing and signing of paper forms). 'In the real world, rolling out these kinds of systems is way more complex,' Wooldridge explains.

We still have some way to go, then, before we work out how best to utilise even the technology that is around us today. Ultimately, it will become an invisible part of our everyday lives. 'There are people there and you need to think about how they fit into the rest of your business,' Wooldridge says. 'It takes time for the technology to become really embedded and for people to find the right way of using it.'

3
Applying AI

Not all AI is equal. Some has reached human standards. Some still has a long way to go. The speech-recognition systems used in Amazon's Echo and Google's Home smart speakers, for example, may have improved to the point where they can be useful to people asking basic questions, but they're still very glitchy. They often mishear or misinterpret basic commands. The technology is improving, but we're far from having voice recognition that can be used for human-like conversations.

By contrast, computer vision and natural-language processing are two areas where AI is currently excelling – to the point where in some cases it's claimed it can perform better than experts who have spent their entire careers working in a given sphere. Both are focused on trying to replicate human behaviour: namely, the ability to see and understand the world around it; and to correctly interpret and reproduce dialects. Thanks to huge new datasets, comprising millions and even trillions of pieces of data, both are making major strides forwards.

Computer vision

Computer vision is much more than simply attaching a camera to a computer. Although we don't fully understand how the human brain processes and comprehends what we see, this field of AI tries to replicate the results. As with the human eye and brain, various stages are involved. A sensor (eyes for a person; some form of camera for a machine) captures data about what is in front of it. This information is passed through an interpretation stage (our brains, or a machine's algorithms) and the end result is that what is seen is understood.

But that's where the similarities stop. Humans are able to see and understand the objects from a very early age: we don't need to be 'told' the difference between a cat and a dog. Machines don't have this inbuilt knowledge, and have to process visual data at a granular level, processing an image rather as they would a barcode.

Depending on their resolution and size, individual images will have hundreds, thousands or even millions of pixels. An image-recognition system sees all these individual pixels as numbers: a white pixel in a black and white photograph may represent a low number, while black could be assigned a high number. The system also recognises bunches of colour, the shapes the pixels make, the distance between these shapes and big changes in the numbers. So, for example, if an image-recognition system is shown a golden Labrador sitting on some grass, it will detect the big change in the numbers assigned to the pixels where the image turns from dark blades of grass to the lighter fur of the dog. Thanks to all the advances made, computer vision can now analyse not only photos but also video footage, enabling it to classify objects (working out a dog is a dog); identify objects (finding a specific pup); and track objects (following that hound as it moves around).

Essentially, there are two main ways to train a machine to do this. With supervised learning, an image-recognition system is trained upon images that are already labelled: in other words, there are tags applied to the objects the system is trying to define. As it analyses thousands or millions of images, it's able to learn the specific features of, say, a dog through seeing patterns in the data. It can then scale up its learning to identify different breeds of dogs or multiple objects, such as cars, lamp posts, and houses, in one image. With unsupervised learning, the machine will learn to group objects that look the same, but will not know what they are due to the lack of labels. This type of approach allows previously unknown patterns in data to be revealed and understood, and it requires less preparatory work on that data as labels do not need to be applied. The results from unsupervised learning can be used in future supervised learning situations.

So advanced is image recognition now that it is on the verge of playing an important role in medical diagnosis. The black and white images taken during medical imaging are one of the key ways in which doctors make their diagnoses. However, in many medical fields, more scans are produced than can quickly be evaluated, and since, of course, diagnosis is reliant on human interpretation and expertise, details can be overlooked and mistakes made. Deep learning, by contrast, can peek inside X-ray or MRI scans and see tiny details that humans tend to miss. It can also do this far faster than a human expert can.

In trials, AI has been shown to be able to detect cancer (including lung, oral, breast, liver, thyroid and dermatological cancers), respiratory conditions including tuberculosis, and eye problems – all from images. In one instance, an MIT deep-learning system was able to predict the presence of breast cancer up to five years before it fully manifested itself by learning what patterns in breast tissue lead to malignant tumours[22] (it learned from scans of 60,000 patients). In another, researchers from Moorfields

Eye Hospital in London, and Google's DeepMind, revealed in the summer of 2018 that Google's system using optical coherence tomography (OCT) scanners, which create 3D models of the eye, could correctly recognise fifty different types of eye disease 94.5 per cent of the time.[23] The AI involved (which used two neural networks) did so by first learning from the data produced by a team of ten expert ophthalmologists and optometrists, who highlighted diseases on image scans, including their specific features. It was then able not only to offer a diagnosis, but also to give it a confidence rating, and mark up the relevant scan to show why it made the decision it had.

'The algorithm is on a par with expert performance at diagnosing OCT scans,' Pearse Keane, a surgeon at Moorfields, told *WIRED* at the time.[24] 'It's as good as, or maybe even a little bit better than, world-leading consultant ophthalmologists at Moorfields in saying what is wrong in these OCT scans.'

A study published in the medical journal the *Lancet* in 2019 summarises the promise of such technology.[25]

Of the 31,587 deep-learning research papers devoted to medical diagnosis and imaging that had been published since 2012, the authors looked at 82 where there was enough data to allow full analysis of the results, and found 'the diagnostic performance of deep-learning models to be equivalent to that of healthcare professionals'. They did, however, issue a caveat: 'More studies considering the integration of such algorithms in real-world settings are needed,' they concluded. The fact is that while the research conducted so far is very promising, these kinds of AI systems need to be proved to work in clinical trials that are thoroughly reviewed and replicated before they can be used on a mass scale. Moving to real-world use requires testing on multiple makes of scanners, ensuring patient conditions are safe and building processes where the technology is used. This is a process that, if done properly and rigorously, could take several years to get results at a wide level. It can be easy to get carried away with the hype. The potential, though, is there.

Medical diagnosis is not the only sphere where image recognition is making strides forward. AI in phone apps now tells those with sight problems what objects are around them. It is used in augmented-reality applications to accurately place digital objects into photos and videos. It can also now group pixels into bigger segments, allowing, for example, all the pixels that make up a human to be identified as one object and be easily recognised.

Object tracking and identification is now far more sophisticated than it was even just a few years ago. A human can be detected as they walk down a street, and their presence can be distinguished from the world around them. Cameras attached to drones can count animals or monitor fruit and vegetables growing in fields to assess how ripe they are. They have been used to assess damaged buildings and structures too unsafe for humans to inspect.

Amazon's experimental cashier-less Go stores make extensive use of object tracking and identification. The computer vision and other sensors they employ can identify a customer by their shape and then track them as they make their way through the store. They can also identify what shoppers put in their baskets.

More generally, computer vision can tell retail stores how many customers are there at any given moment. During the coronavirus pandemic it was used to check whether people were following social-distancing rules. And in broadcasts of football matches it has been employed to follow the ball around the pitch, avoiding the need for expensive crews on site and so allowing more matches to be filmed. It's not infallible, though: in one instance a system was confused by the bald head of a match official and followed it instead of the ball.

In Estonia an AI system that combines satellite data with weather information is monitoring farmers' fields to ensure that they are carrying out any necessary mowing (for which they receive a government subsidy). Ott Velsberg, the country's chief data officer, describes when visiting inspectors would be fobbed off with claims either that the fields had been mowed at the beginning of the season and had grown back or that they were just about to be mowed. 'Even if we had a suspicion that someone was actually not using the government funding as intended, we never got anything back,' he says.

Now, with new images coming in up to every two days, it's possible to keep a constant eye on things and send any necessary notifications to farmers via text or email. Since the project started in 2018, Velsberg says it has already paid for itself, saving officials €665,000 within its first year of use. 'We have actually avoided some potentially negligent use of government subsidies,' he explains. 'One company asked for funding for farmland that was in the middle of a marsh and around it was lakes and rivers. It was inaccessible.' 'The effects have also been kind of not what you only get from the algorithm itself, but to change the mindset of people,' he adds. Thanks to AI's all-seeing presence, there's been a step change in compliance. Satellite-driven AI in Estonia is also now being used to guide ice-breaking vessels, identify tree species, and keep records of forest resources.

Natural language processing

One area of AI in which huge progress has been made is natural language processing. Today, machines can communicate with humans and understand the messages we send them with superhuman speed and accuracy. This has tremendous potential for improving customer service in call centres, but the technology also has implications for society at large. The ability to interact more naturally with computers – and humans – has potentially wide-reaching implications for social, cultural, and economic issues.

With the exception of the first sentence, the paragraph you've just read wasn't written by me. It was written by AI. It may not be absolutely perfect, but it does demonstrate how far the world of natural language processing (NLP) has advanced since it was established in the 1950s. Encompassing everything from language translation to creating summaries of written works, these days NLP technology is at the heart of chatbots, Siri, Alexa and autocomplete systems on phones.

Arguably, no field in AI has benefited from big data quite as much as NLP. The size of the language models created by researchers is, quite simply, colossal. The AI-generated paragraph above, for example, came via the Megatron-11b language model, which has 11 billion parameters. But that's just a drop in the ocean. In the middle of 2020, the San Francisco-based AI lab OpenAI released the latest version of its text generation system: GPT-3. It contained a staggering 175 billion parameters.

GPT-3 is perhaps the most sophisticated language model ever. Feed the system text – be it a couple of sentences or paragraphs – and it will be able to continue the passage in a way that's almost indistinguishable from prose created by humans. If it is told about the style of writing it should produce, it can replicate that style. GPT-3 can write as William Shakespeare – or indeed any historical figure – would have done; it can write creative fiction, and has been experimentally used for content moderation. It's also been used for coding. One developer built a layout generator for a web page that, once given a written description of a particular design, could automatically generate the code to create it. Another developer used it to create a search engine that could answer questions asked of it.

'The results are pretty authentic because it knows about topics beforehand and has been trained on so many things,' says Samanyou Garg, a researcher building an AI email-answering programme and a system to write marketing copy using GPT-3. 'From what I have tested, it is really good at writing text – that could be articles, it could be blog posts, or it could be generating some marketing material.'

As with all deep neural networks the text-generating system works by finding patterns in the data it has been trained on, and making connections between words and how they are used (in GPT-3's case through unsupervised learning). When you type a prompt into it – such as the first sentence of this section – it essentially guesses what words should come next. These aren't random guesses, though: they are based on an informed calculation of the likeliest words to follow.

The system is far from perfect. Ask it a dumb question and it will make up any answer. Every now and again it will throw in sentences that make little sense. There's the chance it can be used to produce fake news and misinformation for those wanting to disrupt society. There's also the danger of it reproducing the human biases in the data it has learned from. Jerome Pesenti, the head of AI at Facebook, tweeted examples of racist and sexist slurs that GPT-3 put out after it was given one-word prompts (such as 'Jews', or '#blacklivesmatter').[26] 'It shouldn't be this easy to generate racist and sexist outputs, especially with neutral prompts,' Pesenti pointed out. (OpenAI quickly introduced a fix that could prevent this happening in the future.)

That said, what excites AI researchers about GPT-3 is the step change it represents. In an earlier iteration it had 1.5 billion parameters, then 117 billion, before it achieved its current 175 billion. Each time it was upgraded, its results improved massively. This suggests that simply increasing the amount of data fed into such systems could move AI closer to general intelligence.

GPT-3 is not the only game in town. Two other significant natural language processing models come from Google (its model is called BERT) and China's Google equivalent, Baidu (its model is called ERNIE). The tongue-in-cheek naming represents both some of the rivalry and familiarity between big tech companies developing AI. Both Google and Baidu have huge resources and knowledge of the internet at their disposal. They've also both successfully used deep learning for translation.

Up until now a vast proportion of NLP research has been focused on the English language. Inevitably, this means that large areas of the world have not been benefiting from NLP models and advances. Africa, for example, has scarcely figured, despite its size, huge global importance and the fact that the continent embraces more than 2,000 languages. Fortunately, the Masakhane project is trying to change that. Calling on the skills of a community of around 400 AI researchers from thirty different African countries, it has produced 49 different translation projects from more than 38 countries, built new datasets and training models, and published its research findings. In doing so, it's had its own challenges to overcome. Bonaventure Dossou, one of the researchers involved, said that during the process of building a dataset for the Fon language, spoken in Benin, he had to create a keyboard on which it could be properly typed. 'Local artists actually are [now] able to write down the lyrics of the songs in Fon,' he says.

It would be wrong to think that adding more languages to translation models simply serves local interests. In fact, it can benefit everyone. Staff at Baidu have found that their AI's understanding of language in general increases as more specific languages are added, learned and translated. 'Mapping any correlation between different languages is an essential component to this process,' says a spokesperson for the company. As of 2020 the company's translation tool supported more than 200 languages and was translating 100 billion characters a day. 'While developing a deep learning-based neural network translation model, we discovered that although languages have huge differences symbolically and grammatically, they can be very similar semantically,' the spokesperson goes on to say. 'On many levels, human cognition, descriptions and expressions of the world are consistent no matter what variation of languages they communicate in.'

The amount of data now being crunched is eye-watering. A research paper about GPT-3 released by OpenAI, for example, shows that the team started with the Common Crawl dataset that's available to researchers.[27] It contains around a trillion words. OpenAI then filtered this for quality and included data from four other datasets, one of which was English-language Wikipedia, which has 6.1 million articles containing more than 3.6 billion words.

Other data was pulled from historical books that are out of copyright and from information drawn from across the web. Millions of web pages and their text were scraped. In fact, any type of writing that you've come across on the English-language internet is likely to have been included within the model (and OpenAI hasn't revealed the full scale of the information it drew on to train GPT-3).

But there's a problem here – and it's one that applies to all deep learning. Processing such vast quantities of data involves the expenditure of enormous amounts of energy. OpenAI admitted as much when it said that its model consumed 'significant resources', although it didn't reveal the potential environmental impact or cost. Unconfirmed estimates put the energy costs of training as being up to $12 million. Whatever the true figure, it's unquestionably the case that larger datasets are on their way, and that they will consume proportionally more energy. Research from the Allen Institute for AI estimated that there was a 300,000 times increase in the computations needed for deep-learning research between 2012 and 2018.[28] 'The problem is getting exponentially worse,' says Oren Etzioni, the CEO of the Institute. 'People have not yet taken this sufficiently seriously.' It raises the question: just how much energy will GPT-10 use?

In June 2019, researchers at the University of Massachusetts Amherst trained four deep-learning language models (GPT-2, Google's BERT, AllenNLP's ELMo and Transformer) for a single day.[29] The power used was multiplied by the time the original creators said their model had needed to be fully trained. They found the models are capable of producing more than five times the equivalent carbon dioxide emissions of an average American car over its entire lifetime, including the manufacturing. 'What's being optimised is really performance on certain datasets,' says Sasha Luccioni, a researcher working on AI and climate change issues at Mila, Université de Montréal. 'They don't even take into consideration how long they run. It's not even a question for a lot of people.'

AI researchers need to change their mindsets when it comes to environmental impact, and the fact is that there are things that can be done. 'You do choose what data you train on, how big your model is, and what data centre you want to choose for training,' Luccioni says. Along with colleagues, Luccioni has built code that can be automatically added to AI models to report on the environmental impact of AI. Called CodeCarbon, it estimates the amount of carbon dioxide (CO_2) produced by computing resources needed in AI models. It does this by automatically detecting the energy grid and hardware used in the training, and it then offers recommendations on how it could be improved. As AI training data becomes even bigger, its energy footprint is something that its developers are going to have to improve.

Self-driving cars

In the spring of 2004, fifteen vehicles were gathered in the Mojave Desert for a unique race. The first vehicle to make it to the finish line 229 kilometres away, navigating through rocky terrain, dips, gullies and unpredictable wildlife, would win the team behind it $1 million. The catch? None of the vehicles was allowed a driver. All had to drive themselves to the end of the race.

Organised by the Defense Advanced Research Projects Agency (DARPA), the contest was the group's first Grand Challenge event. Taking to the start-line were a bunch of *Mad Max*-style vehicles: huge six-wheelers, converted SUVs, and buggies with no driver compartments at all. Hundreds of people filled grandstands around the starting line and witnessed the unfolding spectacle.

As races go it turned out to be a flop. The 'winner' managed to crawl just 11.9 kilometres. Some vehicles barely made it out of the starting funnel. The self-driving cars were confused by bushes; they froze, unable to move forward; they crashed into fences; they got stuck on hills.

Yet in terms of boosting the profile of self-driving vehicle research, the event was a success. A year later five teams completed a similar 212-kilometre course, with the winning team coming over the line in under seven hours.

Nearing two decades on and millions of cars around the world use autonomous driving features – such as lane control and self-parking – and fully autonomous cars have clocked up thousands of kilometres on public roads.

The US Society of Automotive Engineers (SAE) ranks vehicles according to six levels of automation, ranging from no automation at level zero to full automation at level five. Level four vehicles can drive autonomously in most conditions; level five are able to operate autonomously in all conditions. At all levels below four, a driver is required and must remain engaged and ready to take over at any point. During the development stages the AI can be trained in video-game-style simulations, making decisions and then following them through.

The technology and systems needed to create fully self-driving vehicles are similar to those required to build semi-autonomous features that operate at lower levels of the SAE scale. 'Autonomous vehicles are robotic systems, and any robotic system has three major stages. The first stage is sensing, the second is planning, the third is acting,' says Jack Weast, the chief systems architect for Intel's autonomous driving division and a vice-president at the Intel-owned autonomous driving system firm Mobileye.

A key component is computer vision. Cameras positioned around vehicles capture the world around the car, and are able to detect objects and determine what they are. 'You've got sensors with algorithms that are perceiving the environment, classifying objects, understanding what they are, and building a world model, which is this virtual representation of what exists out there in the real world,' Weast says.

Cameras and computer vision aren't the only sensors available. Lidar (using light waves) and radar (radio waves) can be employed, too. Their sensors send out signals that hit objects around a car – from street signs to pedestrians – before they reflect back to the car, building a digital picture of the environment in the process. As radio waves are not as easily absorbed as light waves they can travel over longer distances. The key thing is, whatever combination of sensors and cameras is used, there needs to be plenty of them. 'You need to have redundancy and independence,' says Paul Newman, the founder of the UK-based self-driving software firm Oxbotica. 'Redundancy is multiple cameras, multiple lasers, multiple radars. Independence is, they work in completely different ways.' Only through this combination can safety be ensured. Newman's company is trialling level-four autonomous vehicles on public roads in England. Its autonomous vehicles are also being used in airports and around mines, which pose fewer issues for autonomous vehicles as they are more predictable environments. Since there is a general consensus within the automotive industry that autonomous vehicles will be used at scale in future, everyone from technology companies to traditional vehicle manufacturers is now working on their development. (There are sixty companies holding permits to test autonomous vehicles with human safety drivers in California).

Once signals are received back by a car, along with data from computer vision cameras and any other mapping that's being used, the vehicle is ready to make a virtually instant decision. It is, in fact, constantly sensing and planning its next move. It is observing all the objects around it, from cars and trucks to pedestrians and cyclists, and predicting what they will do next through an assessment of their speed and trajectory.

Within a self-driving vehicle, multiple algorithms and AI systems are at work, alongside non-AI classic statistical approaches. 'In the planning stage, there's a logical block called the driving policy,' says Intel's Jack Weast. This governs how a vehicle should behave. Unlike supervised learning and unsupervised learning, it's based on reinforcement learning that involves a specific goal. The algorithms are told to achieve something – driving economically, for instance – and then attempt to reach it through trial and error. If they succeed, the AI is rewarded, the reward being that the AI is told to replicate more of the correct behaviour it has just demonstrated. 'The reward might be fuel economy, the reward might be safety, the reward might be time to destination,' says

Weast. 'You're trying to optimise for certain things, and so it's a very effective tool for that.'

In terms of making the theory of self-driving a reality, arguably the leading company is Waymo, an offshoot of Google that was started within the tech giant's research labs in 2009. In the course of a decade, the company's self-driving system has allowed its vehicles to travel more than 30 million kilometres on public roads. Most has been done with a safety driver sitting behind the wheel, ready to take control of the car if it looks as though things are going wrong. But, since 2015, some journeys have been undertaken without a safety driver present. According to the company, as of early 2020, 1,000–2,000 autonomous rides were being operated a week in a 260-square-kilometre area of Phoenix, Arizona, of which up to 10 per cent were fully driverless. In all, in the first nine months of 2020, 105,000 kilometres of fully autonomous driving was achieved.

The day when fully self-driving vehicles are being used commercially at scale is, however, still some way off. There are legal questions to be overcome. Who is at fault when a fully autonomous car crashes? Is it the hardware or software maker? There are practical issues. How will it work when, say, 50 per cent of all vehicles on the road are autonomous and the remainder are driven by humans who refuse to embrace the technology? And there are the inevitable trust and safety questions. Can a machine make the right decision every time? How safe can it really be?

Fatal accidents involving semi-autonomous cars are certainly not unknown. In March 2018, for example, an Apple employee who was using one of Tesla's semi-autonomous driving features died after his car smashed into a concrete barrier. The US National Transportation Safety Board investigated and ended up pinning the blame on both driver and vehicle.[30] It concluded that the driver was playing a game at the time of the accident, that he didn't have his hands on the wheel as the system required and that he was 'over-reliant' on the software.[31] It also judged that Tesla's collision system did not detect

69

the crash barrier the car hit, and that it didn't effectively monitor the driver's engagement with the road.

Google's Waymo has released some details about the number of crashes its self-driving vehicles have been involved in over the course of journeys totalling 9.8 million kilometres[32] (for 105,000 kilometres of which, as previously mentioned, human safety drivers were not present). It's a relatively small dataset, but nevertheless provides an interesting insight into the sort of challenges that self-driving vehicles face. Overall, it emerges, there were forty-seven collision or contact 'events'. Eighteen of these actually occurred. The other twenty-nine events would have occurred, according to later Waymo simulations, had a human not intervened. In sixteen events, Waymo cars were rear-ended, eight of these being when the Waymo car was already stopped for a traffic light. In other incidents, people walked or rode their bikes into the autonomous vehicle; others broke driving laws before hitting it; a head-on incident was caused by a non-autonomous car travelling in the wrong lane. A Waymo car was responsible for hitting another vehicle just once. 'Nearly all the actual and simulated events involved one or more road rule violations or other incautious behaviour by another agent,' its teams wrote in a research paper about its crashes. 'AVs will share roads with human drivers for the foreseeable future, and significant numbers of collisions due to human driver errors that are simply unavoidable should be expected during this period.'

Such a diagnosis would appear to confirm the view of proponents of self-driving technology that it is actually safer than conventional transport. After all, millions of people die in regular car crashes around the world every year. Jack Weast says that Intel's approach when it comes to safety is to use a deterministic approach – rather than a machine basing its decisions on how much of a probability the AI thinks things will happen. 'It's like a checker on the decisions that the AI is recommending, so when, inevitably, this probabilistic algorithm recommends something that might not be good for safety, we have a deterministic way to check is that a safe action or not,' he says.

Self-driving cars certainly do have some big advantages over humans. They are able to sense things around them faster, and are able to look in all directions at once. Their reaction times are also faster. And they don't get tired. 'The single thing that we screw up as humans is we lose concentration,' says Paul Newman. 'We just get distracted. And that's the single thing a machine won't do. How many accidents are caused by fatigue and stupid stuff?'

Moreover, self-driving cars can learn from each other. Oxbotica's AI systems that underpin how its vehicles operate are refreshed every night. All the new data and new scenarios that the vehicles have found themselves in – both in the real world and in virtual simulations – can be added to the systems' knowledge. In one day hundreds of hours of new experiences and knowledge can be added to a vehicle's understanding of how to drive. Every car can have the experience of every other car – and when there are thousands or millions of vehicles operating each day this pooled understanding grows exponentially.

Technologists believe the way machines like this can function in the real world is through explaining to people how they actually work and the benefits they can have. 'We need to move away from saying these things are somehow spooky and not explainable,' adds Newman. 'They are engineered pieces of software, there is process around them and we can say how we expect them to behave.'

4
AI's pitfalls

Between 2015 and 2020 people applying for visas to enter the United Kingdom to work, study or visit loved ones would fill in the paperwork in the usual way, and that data would then be handed over to an algorithm to assess. It would give them a rating: red, amber or green. Of those being assessed as green 96.3 per cent were waved through. Those marked as red – the 'riskiest' category – weren't automatically rejected, but were subject to further checks, with senior staff being brought in to check the data and make a final decision. This partially automated process, run by the Home Office, ultimately approved 48 per cent of red applications. Those using it trusted its decisions.

But there was a problem. Although the intention behind the system was laudable – to make visa applications faster, more efficient and less bureaucratic – the underlying technology, known as the streaming tool, was flawed. It was plagued with data, transparency and process problems that resulted in unfair decisions. In particular, it judged people to be high-risk on the basis of their country of origin rather than on carefully considered personal criteria. 'They kept this list of undesirable nations where simply by making an application coming from a particular country – and they refused to give us the name of the countries – that person would be more likely to be streamed amber or red,' says Cori Crider, the founder of legal group Foxglove.

In the spring of 2020 Foxglove challenged the algorithmic process, arguing that it broke equality and data protection laws. Days before the case was due to reach court the UK government scrapped the tool, admitting it needed to scrutinise 'issues around unconscious bias and the use of nationality generally in the streaming tool'. However, it rejected the suggestions that the system was breaking any laws.

Months later, in the midst of the coronavirus pandemic, a similar algorithm attempted to predict English students'

A-Level exam grades. It, too, used historical data to make decisions about individuals' futures. It, too, was flawed. Widespread protest ensued, with students taking to the streets and chanting 'Fuck the algorithm'.

Neither system involved particularly complex algorithms – and neither used artificial intelligence. But what they both demonstrate is the inherently risky nature of data. Whatever we might be tempted to assume, it is rarely, if ever, neutral. Since it is ultimately created by humans, it captures our prejudices. The visa system was founded on data that made biased assumptions about people's countries of origin. The exams system predicted results based in part on the previous track record of individual pupils' schools. Both are warnings for the future.

Bias

Since data lies at the heart of AI, it follows that AI is not free from prejudice. Bad data put into a system results in bad data outputs. There are three common forms of bias – although research has identified more than 20 types of bias, plus other types of discrimination and unfairness that can be present in AI setups. With *latent bias*, an algorithm correlates its results with such characteristics in the data as gender, race, income and more, so potentially perpetuating historical forms of bias: for example, a system may 'learn' that doctors are male because the historical data it has been trained on shows doctors as being male. (Amazon had to scrap an AI hiring tool it was using, which was trained upon ten years of CV data, as the system surmised that since men had historically been hired more often than women, they must be better.) With *selection bias* results are distorted by a dataset that over-represents one group of people. (An AI created to judge a beauty contest selected mostly white winners, as the dataset it was trained upon mostly contained images of white people.) With *interaction bias* a system learns from the prejudices people display when they interact with it. (Microsoft's chatbot, Tay, which was launched on Twitter in 2016, became more coherent within its first twenty-four hours of use, but also repeated all the sexist and racist language people had sent its way.)

All these biases show the risks of using data to predict future outcomes. And within AI the problem has been pronounced. Take law enforcement, for example. In the US in particular the police have come to use predictive systems when they're seeking to assess how likely someone is to re-offend, or whether they should be granted bail, or when spikes in crimes are likely to happen. The trouble is that such systems inevitably target individuals and communities that have historically been the focus of particular police attention. 'If you're using problematic data, you're going to get problematic policing,' explains Renée Cummings, a researcher specialising in AI in the criminal justice sector and its discriminatory effects. In the US people who are black are more than twice as likely to be arrested as white people. They are more likely to be stopped without cause by police, and black men are 2.5 times more likely to be killed by police than white men. 'It starts from a place of bias,' Cummings says. 'AI has really amplified the biases and the discrimination that has been a part of the system.'

A 2016 investigation by ProPublica revealed how predictive software, called COMPAS, was biased against black people.[33] A further study of the tool, which can determine risk, found that it is 'not well calibrated for Hispanics.'[34] It was said to over-predict risk scores for Hispanic people and was marked by an inability to make accurate predictions. AI can also perpetuate police misdemeanours. A study by researchers at New York University's AI Now Institute of thirteen US jurisdictions where predictive policing tools have been in operation concluded that 'illegal police practices can significantly distort the data that is collected, and the risks that dirty data will still be used for law enforcement and other purposes.'[35]

Even when race data is stripped from predictive policing AI systems (a frequent requirement of equalities laws), problems remain. Rashida Richardson, the author of the AI Now paper, who is now a visiting scholar at Rutgers Law School, points out that there are numerous forms of data that can serve as proxies for race. Location is one. If you live in an area that is already heavily policed because of its racial composition, it follows that there will be more police reports on file and so a great likelihood of AI deeming your area to be crime-ridden. Other data profiles that can lead to distortion include age and social links. One predictive policing tool used in the Netherlands employs demographic data such as the number of one-parent households, the number of people receiving social benefits, and the number of non-Western immigrants as factors in determining how likely a crime is to happen in a particular area.[36] The problem with all this is that while the data collected may sometimes contain useful pointers, it is not neutrally predictive. 'Police data is more likely to reflect the practices, policies and priorities of a police department and environment of policing than necessarily crime trends,' Richardson explains. She questions whether predictive policing technologies are a reflection of what happens in communities: 'The reality is, if it's relying mostly on police data, which often is not collected for the subsequent use for some type of data analysis, then it's always going to have some type of permanent flaw in it that makes it hard to use for any purpose in policing.'

There is currently little evidence to demonstrate that predictive or AI risk assessment tools actually work. Studies showing that algorithmic decision tools can make better predictions than humans are few in number, and because police forces are generally tight-lipped about their use of AI technologies their data has not often been independently analysed and verified. However, one Los Angeles Police Department review of a system called PredPol, which is used in multiple places across the US, said it was 'difficult to draw conclusions about the effectiveness of the system in reducing vehicle or other crime'.[37]

In June 2020, more than 1,400 mathematicians signed an open letter stating that they did not believe the field should be collaborating with police on these systems.[38] It also demanded that audits be introduced for those systems already in place. 'It is simply too easy to create a scientific veneer for racism,' the researchers wrote. Cori Crider, who led the legal challenges to flawed statistical systems in the UK, adds that these types of technologies often seem to be used against groups who may not have the means to challenge them. 'It feels like a lot of the systems are directed at the management and mass management of people who have much less power, social capital, money, all of the rest of it,' she says. 'I think that there is a really worrying trend, in that algorithmic management is a way to contain and surveil poor people of colour.'

It's not just policing where AI bias can rear its head. Housing, employment and financial matters have all suffered from bias problems. Healthcare is emerging as the newest sector to suffer with issues. In the US, for instance, researchers from the University of California, Berkeley, discovered that an algorithm used by insurers and hospitals to manage the care of around 200 million people a year gave lower risk scores to people who self-identified as black than to white people who were equally sick.[39] This was because it determined people's health scores in part according to how much they had spent on healthcare in a year, the assumption being that sicker people spend more than healthy ones. However, the data also showed there was $1,800 less per year of care given to black patients than to white patients with the same number of chronic health problems. 'Less money is spent on Black patients who have the same level of need, and the algorithm thus falsely concludes that Black patients are healthier than equally sick White patients,' the authors of the study wrote. As a result black people were less likely to be referred for treatments involving more specialist care. Had it been a level playing field, 46.5 per cent of the black patients involved would have been referred. As it was, the percentage stood at 17.7 per cent.

As AI becomes more sophisticated, researchers worry that the connections made by algorithms will become more obscure. Proxies for certain types of data will become harder to identify, and machines may make links between certain types of information that humans don't associate together, or can't see because of the scale of the information being crunched. The first signs of this happening are already evident.

In March 2019, for example, the US Department of Housing and Urban Development (HUD) charged Facebook with discrimination over how its targeted advertising for housing works.[40] US advertising laws prohibit discrimination against people based on their colour, race, national origin, sex, religion, disability and family status, and, while Facebook's system wasn't explicitly guilty of such discrimination, it emerged that the interests people had, as expressed online, led to their exclusion from particular ads.

'An algorithm is grouping people not based necessarily on sexual orientation or their skin colour,' says Sandra Watcher, associate professor and senior research fellow in the law and ethics of AI at the Oxford

Internet Institute. She says algorithms group people with similar behaviours. 'These similarities could be that they all have green shoes, or similarities could be that they eat Indian food on a Tuesday, or that they play video games.' The problem is that such correlations can lead to wholly false inferences – an algorithm might, for example, conclude that people who wear green shoes do, or don't, have a tendency to repay their loans on time. To any human, such a conclusion would be preposterous. To an AI it may seem entirely logical.

'Even if a bank can explain which data and variables have been used to make a decision (e.g. banking records, income, postcode), the decision turns on inferences drawn from these sources; for example, that the applicant is not a reliable borrower,' Watcher writes.[41] 'This is an assumption or prediction about future behaviour that cannot be verified or refuted at the time of decision-making.' She argues that data protection laws need to evolve to handle the issues that arise when machines make false deductions about us. Organisations using such systems should have to prove the connections they are making are reasonable: they should say why certain data is relevant, why the inferences matter to the decision that's being made and whether the process is accurate and reliable. If not, Watcher says, more people will suffer at the hands of AIs issuing unfair decisions.

Surveillance

If AI has proved problematic when it's crunching data, it's also displayed severe shortcomings when it's processing images involving humans – particularly through facial-recognition technology.

How these systems work is quite simple, at least in theory. If, say, a surveillance camera linked to an AI system detects a face, measurements between facial features, such as the distance between the forehead and chin, are taken and a biometric map is created. This map is used to create a faceprint (in reality, a series of numbers). This is then compared against other faceprints in the database for a possible match. The underlying algorithms have been trained on matching faces to others in datasets.

Police forces around the world use such AI to detect people already logged on their systems as criminals or potential criminals. If there's a match when a live deployment is being used, officers on the ground are alerted and can track the suspect down. Some cameras running live facial-recognition systems are clearly marked. But many of the more sophisticated models look much like any other CCTV cameras. One particularly advanced series of cameras, launched in 2020, which uses six AI algorithms, offers up to 12-megapixel resolution and combines facial recognition with crowd counting and car number plate reading. It can monitor perimeters and queues, and can even detect if people are wearing hard hats or not.

That, at least, is the theory. In practice, high levels of accuracy in lab tests are often not replicated in the real world. Low light levels can play havoc with facial recognition, as can poor-quality video footage. The sun can be a particular pain. In an early trial of live facial-recognition systems by police in the UK, 2,470 faces were judged to be matches with those held in the police database. In fact, only 8 per cent were. All the other so-called matches turned out to be false ones.

Accuracy is a problem. Because many systems have been trained predominantly on images of white people, they tend to be less accurate when it comes to detecting black and brown faces. Incorrect identifications have therefore been made. In January 2020, 41-year-old Robert Williams, a black man from Michigan, spent thirty hours in custody thanks to an algorithm sparking a wrongful arrest.[42] Another black man, 26-year-old Michael Oliver from Detroit, is suing police over a similar misidentification.[43]

There are privacy issues, too. CCTV cameras are now ubiquitous, and we have very little say over where they are placed or how their images are used. In time they can be upgraded to use facial recognition. Police forces claim that facial recognition can make our lives safer, and that they are an important weapon in the fight against crime. But such advantages have to be balanced with civil liberty considerations. In the UK, several people have been stopped and challenged over their decision to cover their faces rather than have them scanned by surveillance technology. A teenager was stopped after they had already been dealt with by the courts (an out-of-date database was to blame here).[44] A danger is that because surveillance is now so widespread it has become normalised. Many people are familiar with home security cameras fitted with motion detection – most popularly from Amazon-owned Ring – so they may well regard surveillance as a beneficial part of everyday life. Such people tend to live in more affluent neighbourhoods where homeowners are least likely to be misidentified by the technology, so they're less aware of the dangers. But that doesn't mean the downsides don't exist.

It's perhaps at a national level that the positive and negatives of a surveillance world are most apparent.

Certainly it's at a national level that the true extent of its power is most clear. Take the way India used surveillance AI during the early weeks of the coronavirus pandemic in April 2020. As the first wave spread, police forces in Delhi and Mumbai sent up drones to monitor people, to enforce the national lockdown and to improve social distancing (a local start-up in Mumbai contributed by donating 45 drones). Onboard cameras captured footage of potentially illegal gatherings and speakers blared out messages ordering groups to disperse. Police viewing the video in real time could scramble officers to where they were needed.

Meanwhile, in Amritsar, the second-largest city in the state of Punjab, airborne surveillance was supercharged. The start-up Skylark Labs flew drones that used computer vision to detect precisely how close to one another people were standing (a green bounding box would appear around them if they were far enough apart, and a red one if they were too close). 'There's a mapping algorithm, which divides the map of the whole city into ten grids, and we just tell them [the police] to select the grids where they want to fly – and the drones would automatically take off and fly in that grid,' explains Amarjot Singh, the CEO of Skylark. 'If a human was detected, it would flag the human, and it would send a message onto the phone of police officers who were close to that area,' he adds. The system was then rolled out to a further six cities. Two hundred fines were ultimately issued and some cars impounded. The use of the technology sets worrying new precedents for government control of citizens – people's behaviour is quietly watched from above.

India is not the only country where such intrusive surveillance is being deployed by state and local governments. 'There are more countries out there that are experimenting with procuring and purchasing and investing in these systems than I expected,' says Steven Feldstein, a senior fellow in Carnegie's Democracy, Conflict, and Governance Program. He conducted the first review of how AI surveillance – smart city systems, facial recognition and smart policing set-ups – is used around the world. By the summer of 2020, he estimated, seventy-seven countries out of 179 were deploying such technologies.[45] They range from liberal democracies, such as the UK and US, to the autocratic regimes of Russia and Saudi Arabia. Feldstein noted a particular link between investment in surveillance and countries with high military budgets.

And the technology is growing in range and ambition. People can now be identified from their irises, their tattoos, the way they walk (gait recognition technology), and more. Soon there will be no place to hide. Researchers in China and the UK have built a system that's able to identify people over a series of weeks, even if they've changed their clothing and hairstyle.[46] Work is also under way to create systems that claim to calculate people's emotions or feelings based on their facial expressions. (Experts say this ambition is flawed and question whether the technology should even exist in the first place). Much of all this is still in the experimental, laboratory phase, but it gives a good sense of the overall direction of technological travel. And it's being fed by ever greater quantities of training data, more sophisticated hardware, and improved machine-learning algorithms.

Some authorities are treating such advances with caution. In the US, facial-recognition systems have been banned in some states, with the city of Portland, Oregon, adopting the most thorough-going ban (even businesses there are not allowed to use the technology). The EU has reportedly been mulling similar restrictions. In nations such as India, on the other hand, the technology is getting an ever-greater hold. Officials there boasted that it was instrumental in identifying 1,100 people involved in violent riots in Delhi over two days in February 2020. 'This is a software. It does not see faith. It does not see clothes. It only sees the face, and through the face the person is caught,' Indian government minister Amit Shah was reported as saying, when asked about innocent people being monitored by the cameras.[47]

The country that constitutes the most extreme test case for the technology is China. No other nation has been as enthusiastic in the pursuit of surveillance systems as this communist superstate. It routinely harvests huge amounts of data about its citizens and has widely implemented facial-recognition technology. 'The China model is pretty distinctive,' says Steven Feldstein. 'No other country really comes close in terms of replicating or even having an aspiration to undertake total surveillance along the lines of what they do.' The country is also the world's biggest exporter of AI surveillance technology. Feldstein estimates that Huawei, Hikvision, Dahua, and ZTE supply tech to 63 countries. Huawei alone supplies technology to 50 countries – a long way ahead of the next largest non-Chinese firm, Japan's NEC (which is used in 14 countries).

One study, conducted by researchers from the Shanghai Research Institute, and published in June 2020, gives a sense of what a dystopian future might hold if the technology is left unchecked. The study utilised a network of security cameras, along with other sensors (which measured movement, temperature and so on), in

100,000 lifts across China, and fed the data into multiple algorithms to help determine when people's behaviour was not 'normal'.[48] The intention was to detect potentially unsafe behaviour (the researchers report being paid by a client to use the technology to try to detect any instances of illegal over-crowding in some blocks of flats). But it also had aspirations of determining people's gender, age, appearance and occupation. And potentially unsafe behaviour included not just 'overcrowded residence' but 'drug dealing, pyramid sale gathering, prostitution' – presumably the list could have been extended further.

Each time a lift stopped at a floor, a photo was taken. 'There are around one million records for each floor from 100,000 elevators,' the researchers say in their paper. Overall, 643 instances of people behaving potentially abnormally were detected. Of these, more than 100 were down to errors with equipment, or images gathered from the security cameras on the network that weren't in blocks of flats (such as cameras in shopping mall elevators, or office buildings). In 289 cases the researchers decided 'something different is there' and determined that the building manager should try to find out more details. The research says three of the flagged incidents appeared to show people running catering services out of their flats; six incidents hinted at over-crowding.

Despite the scale on which it operated, the system was relatively rudimentary. It wasn't working in real time, and the sheer size of the data gathered meant that the researchers didn't analyse people's ages and possible occupations. But the potential was there. And that potential – not just to detect wrong-doing but to snoop on and control people who have done nothing wrong – has worrying implications for every aspect of everyday existence, from the daily routines of home life to monitoring how productive people are at work and setting targets for them, to keeping an eye on us in shops and in airports.

One repressive instance of mass surveillance that critics of the Chinese regime would point to concerns the country's largely Muslim minority group the Uighurs. In one area, for just one month during 2019, facial recognition was used 500,000 times to screen whether people moving past cameras were Uighur, the *New York Times* reported.[49] 'If originally one Uighur lives in a neighborhood, and within twenty days six Uighurs appear,' the paper reported one company saying, 'it immediately sends alarms' to local police. Such technological ability will only increase in the future.

Deepfakes

Towards the end of 2017, an anonymous Reddit user changed the online world. Posting under the moniker 'deepfakes', they started sharing pornographic videos of celebrities, using deep learning to replace the faces of the original performers with those of the famous. Taylor Swift, Gal Gadot, Maisie Williams and Scarlett Johansson were just some of the victims. Since then, deepfakes have become far-reaching.

Photoshopping has, of course, been around for decades. But deepfakes are far more sophisticated and can be just as convincing. Rather than simply relying on a human agent to fit images from different sources together, they feed original footage through an AI program that is able to use the data supplied to generate new data. Generative adversarial networks (GANs), created in 2014, are the commonest tool in use in this sphere. The larger the dataset with which they are supplied, the more realistic the images they generate.

Deepfakes are yet another instance of the challenges to society that AI poses. Their use can be entirely innocent. But they can also cause real harm. And the technology behind them has come a long way since the first poor-quality images created on Reddit. It's growing exponentially and is being democratised in the process through freely available online tutorials and open-sourced code. In July 2019 the deepfake detection cybersecurity company Sensity found 14,678 deepfakes online.[50] By June 2020 the number had increased to 49,081. Most are pornographic; most target women. Sensity's June 2020 figures revealed that 1,000 deepfake pornographic videos were being uploaded to mainstream adult video sites every month, gathering millions of views.[51] To make matters worse, there are currently no laws in place that can tackle the problem. Victims are left having to navigate existing copyright, defamation and human rights laws in their bids to get non-consensual deepfakes of themselves removed from the internet.

It's not just a problem for movie stars and musicians. YouTubers, Instagram stars and women who stream on Twitch have also been targeted by the technology. In October 2020 it was revealed that an AI bot on the messaging platform Telegram was using deepfake technology to 'strip' the clothes from photos of women and generate naked body parts in their place. More than 100,000 women had been victims. Most of those creating the images say they used the technology against women they knew.[52]

The fact is that the tentacles of online faking are reaching ever further. During the summer of 2019, for example, journalists working for AP found a faked LinkedIn account, with connections to leading influential US figures, was using a profile image developed by a GAN. 'We encounter them very frequently on LinkedIn and Twitter, not even with us looking for them, we just come across these,' explains Henry Ajder, at the time of speaking a threat intelligence researcher at Sensity. 'These images are super-readily available, they are incredibly easy to access.' In December 2019 Facebook removed pages originating in Georgia and Vietnam that Sensity confirmed had used fake images as profile pictures.[53] In August 2020 Facebook itself said it had removed 13 account profiles it believed to have originated in Russia that it deemed 'likely' to have used GANs to create their images.[54] Such fakes are getting easier to produce. Nvidia's open-sourced StyleGAN and StyleGAN2 face-generation software, which uses GANs, is free for anyone to use and can easily be used to create images of fictional people. (You can test whether you can tell the difference between real and AI-generated images of people on whichfaceisreal.com).

Audio is being similarly manipulated and it can help with financial scams. Cybersecurity company NISOS documented a case (with accompanying audio evidence) from June 2020 when an employee at a tech firm received a voicemail, apparently from their CEO, asking for an urgent payment to be made.[55] Fortunately the fake wasn't quite good enough to fool the employee because the voice wasn't sufficiently close to the CEO's. NISOS's analysis subsequently revealed that the audio was also too choppy, that the high notes peaked too often, and that the background noise one would expect on a normal call was lacking. But then this is the first case to have been fully described. Future efforts will doubtlessly be more believable.

As for AI-generated text, a US college student, Liam Porr, reported using GPT-3 to create blog posts that went on to be read 26,000 times within two weeks of their online publication.[56] One post even ended up at the top of the news aggregation site and forum Hacker News. Porr said that only a couple of people – from a tech-literate community who were aware of GPT-3 – actually questioned whether the text they were reading was written by a human.

At the moment the quality of synthetic media varies considerably. Even so it can prove persuasive, particularly among people who are socially or politically biased in favour of the message it is pedalling. A video of Nancy Pelosi, the Speaker of the United States House of Representatives, which had been deliberately slowed down to make her appear drunk, was viewed millions of times after its release in May 2019. In Gabon in early 2019, a video of the country's president – which some called a deepfake although no researchers were able to conclusively prove it either way – led to military unrest.[57]

Once synthetic media is supercharged it will inevitably be even harder to spot. Software tools will make it easy for anyone to manipulate video, text, audio and images convincingly. Efforts are being made by researchers to develop AI tools to spot deepfakes, but these have a long way to go. It seems inevitable that laws will need to be updated to offer better protection to individuals, that social media platforms will need to enforce robust policies, and that those who are the victims of malicious synthetic media will be able to win full recourse.

And there's no doubt that supercharged synthetic media is on its way. According to a report from Samsung Next, the investment arm of the South Korean tech giant, more than 170 start-ups working in the AI synthetic media landscape were in operation in November 2020. They ranged from companies such as Sensity, which is trying to mitigate the threat of synthetic media, to firms working on generating new content to be used in videos, audio recordings, advertising, apps and much more. Some are trying to build AI systems that can read out loud in the same natural way humans do, complete with pauses and expression. Others are seeking to turn written news articles into videos hosted by AI news anchors, to swap people's faces into their favourite movie scenes, and to create realistic avatars that can be used in the multi-billion-dollar gaming industry.

AI is making its way in Hollywood, too. The movie industry has been using CGI and visual effects for decades. Synthetic video offers studios the possibility of being able to cut down on filming costs and use performers in new ways. That's still some way off, but Victor Riparbelli, the CEO of synthetic video company Synthesia, predicts that 'In ten years' time, I think you can produce a Hollywood film on a laptop.'

Such potential advances serve as a reminder that, as with all technology in general, and AI in particular, synthetic media carries great promise as well as posing challenges and threats. Even now, some of the ways in which it is being used show that it is capable of much more than fake footage and dishonest messaging. In February 2020, during an Indian election campaign in Delhi, Manoj Tiwari, the president of the Bharatiya Janata Party (BJP), was able to reach an estimated 15 million people by releasing two videos: one in which he spoke in English, the other in which a dubbing artist impersonated Tiwari and a lip-sync algorithm then altered his mouth to allow

Tiwari to appear to be communicating in fluent Haryanvi, a Hindi dialect.[58] 'Deepfake technology has helped us scale campaign efforts like never before,' Neelkant Bakshi, a campaign manager for BJP, told *Vice*. In much the same way Synthesia has used its AI to make footballer David Beckham appear to speak in nine different languages as he promoted an education awareness campaign for a charity working to eradicate malaria.[59]

Riparbelli says much of Synthesia's work in the near future will focus on turning text into information videos. 'You can imagine if you're a big company with lots of retail workers, sending out a five-page PDF document on new security guidelines, it's not an effective way to communicate with them,' he explains. AI can turn these documents into an engaging video. 'We see ourselves not as a replacement for normal video – this is not something which you buy to save money in a video production. This is an alternative to text.'

Riparbelli is quick to point out that synthetic media cannot possibly work in all situations. It's unlikely, for example, that anyone would respond kindly to a one-on-one meeting with their boss that actually involves chatting to a synthetic video powered by an AI chatbot. He also thinks transparency is essential: 'I think a lot of the places where you've got to be served synthetic videos, it's going to be obvious that it's a synthetic video.' If that can be achieved more generally, then some of the currently problematic aspects of synthetic media will be considerably mitigated.

5

AI and the world of work

If you want to get a sense of where AI is now, and where it's heading next, Ocado Technology is not a bad place to start. At the warehouses of the British online grocery tech company, robots, guided by AI, whizz around on rails at speeds of up to four metres per second, picking a 50-item order in minutes. The journeys then taken by Ocado's delivery trucks are optimised by a neural network that makes more than 14 million last-mile routing calculations per second, and adjusts delivery routes each time a customer places a new order or adds extra items to their shopping lists.

But Ocado's most ambitious automation efforts involve packing robots. At the time of writing the company has five robotic picking arms powered by computer vision, and other machine-learning systems that can identify the products that need to be packed and use suction power to grab them. Further advances, undertaken in conjunction with two European academic-led projects, are in the pipeline.

Picking and packing aren't easy if you're a robot. 'From a human's perspective, it is a fairly simple task to pick and pack, and it doesn't require an awful lot of training,' says Alex Harvey, chief of advanced technology at Ocado Technology. 'For a computer and for a robot, the dexterous manipulation involved is far beyond the state of the art today to be able to pick and pack the full range of items that we do.'

Ocado's Robotic Suction Pick (RSP) machine is a vacuum cup, powered by an air compressor, that sits at the end of an articulated arm. It uses computer vision and built-in sensors to select items gathered by a bot and place them into a shopping bag. Ocado.com sells a vast range of products, running into the tens of thousands. In terms of outward physical appearance, some are much the same: a tin of chopped tomatoes, for example, is not that different from a tin of lentils. But a tin of chopped tomatoes is very different indeed from a pack of yoghurts, which in turn are more sturdy than, say, a bunch of grapes. And, of course, even grapes aren't all the same – they vary according to their variety and state of ripeness. Get the pressure of the vacuum cup wrong and the RSP will either drop or crush the item it is attempting to manipulate. Get the sequence wrong and there's a danger that the tin of tomatoes will squash the grapes.

At present, the company is expanding the number of items its robotic suction system can pick. 'There's no point having for sixty thousand different items, sixty thousand different control pieces of code,' Harvey says. 'What we want at Ocado is generalised control strategies.' But challenges remain. 'We need to fit a robot into the same square footage that the person sits in or operates in, and we need the robot system to achieve the same throughput.' Until a robot can pick and pack as many items in an hour as a human being – Harvey says this is around 600–700 items – it is unlikely to be widely adopted: the impact on productivity would damage service and profits. It also has to be affordable, which means, on the one hand, scaling the technology to the point where it becomes economically worthwhile, and, on the other hand, not over-speccing it (for example, by using a camera with an unnecessarily high resolution). 'When we're deploying stuff in the real world, we want it to be economical in the way that we're deploying it,' Harvey says. 'I don't want to deploy a supercomputer next to every robot picker.'

Whether or not such AI will ultimately replace humans is the billion-dollar question. Many now believe AI will work alongside humans. Obviously, AI offers the promise of greater efficiency, but so far, at least, this tends to hold good only where the environment is relatively controlled and predictable. Production lines and warehouses may well become fully automated. But where processes interact with the outside world – with all its randomness – it's harder to envisage a wholly AI future. Delivery drivers, for instance, have to take into account such factors as the weather and the erratic behaviour of some pedestrians. It's possible that there will be a future without them. It's also possible, though, that AI will control lorries and delivery trucks on major highways where conditions are relatively predictable, and that human drivers will take over the driving as they reach the outskirts of the villages, towns and cities set as their destinations.

Arguably, it's the medical sphere where AI's potential and its limitations have been most apparent – and where its possible future relationship with humans has been most clearly demonstrated. Take Google's computer-vision system, for example. It's capable of spotting diabetic retinopathy, a complication of diabetes that can cause sight loss. In lab conditions, it can achieve an accuracy rate of 90 per cent and provide results in ten minutes.

When put to a real-world test in Thailand, however, the deep-learning set-up often struggled.[60] The 11 clinics that operated it used different technology. Only two had a dedicated eye-screen room that could be made dark enough for patients' pupils to enlarge to the point where high-quality fundus photos could be taken. Most had to make use of nurses' offices or general-purpose rooms. Emma Beede, the lead Google Health researcher evaluating the technology, described one room where, because dental checks and patient consultation were going on, it was essential to leave the light on. 'That makes sense for them,' she said. 'That makes sense when you're under-resourced.' Poor internet connection caused problems, too – at one clinic it dropped out altogether for two hours. One way and another, during the first six months of the trial, 21 per cent (393) of the 1,838 images put through the system proved to be of an insufficiently high quality. Nurses and patients felt frustrated. 'I'll do two tries,' one nurse said. 'The patients can't take more than that.'

And then there was the human factor. At one clinic half the patients earmarked for the study declined to be involved after finding out that although the results would be virtually instantaneous (previously some results had taken ten weeks to arrive), a positive diagnosis would see them being referred to a hospital an hour's drive away. One member of medical staff told the Google researchers that patients 'are not concerned with accuracy, but how the experience will be – will it waste my time if I have to go to the hospital?'

There's little doubt that the technology works: tests in the trial proved accurate when conditions were right. And when things were going well, Beede says, senior nurses felt they had more time to spend with patients and speak to them about their health and lifestyles. But the unpredictability of the everyday world and the needs and concerns of humans cannot be ignored. 'I think the main takeaway from this research is that we need to be designing AI tools with people at the centre,' says Beede. 'We need to be considering our success beyond the accuracy of the model. We need to understand how it's actually going to work for real people in context.' She argues that as more AI is implemented in the real world, more pilot studies will be required to ensure that it works for everyone involved. 'That implementation is of equal importance to the accuracy of the algorithm itself, and cannot always be controlled through careful planning,' the Google report concludes.

The need for a proper and carefully considered partnership between humans and AI has been well demonstrated by Finale Doshi-Velez, a Harvard University computer science professor who leads its Data to Actionable Knowledge Lab. In one experiment, she and her colleagues recruited 220 psychiatrists to study case notes for hypothetical patients supposedly suffering from major depressive disorder.[61] Each set of case notes described that particular patient's condition and was then followed by either an independently verified correct AI-generated recommendation for treatment, an incorrect recommendation or no recommendation at all. Where an AI diagnosis was given, it was accompanied by an explanation for that diagnosis, which varied in length, quality and detail.

'What we found was that when the recommendation was correct, overall, everything improved,' Doshi-Velez says. Doctors and AI decisions proved to be a formidable team. 'Humans may have already had an idea, the recommendation reinforced it or caused them to change their mind to that idea.' However, when the recommendation presented to the volunteer doctors was incorrect, it tended to lead to poorer forms of decision-making. The psychiatrists were influenced by incorrect recommendations from the AI, leading to lower levels of treatment selection accuracy. This is scarcely a new phenomenon. It's long been known that if we put machines in charge of simple tasks, humans will, without continuous training, forget how to do them. Hence, at an everyday level, why digital contact books in phones have caused us not to remember phone numbers any more. Hence, at an extreme level, why on 1 June 2009 the pilots of Air France Flight 447, who had come to rely heavily on the plane's autopilot features, could not cope when the systems failed, and so presided over a crash in which 228 people perished. With AI this 'paradox of automation' is only going to become more pronounced.

The way in which information is presented is also an important factor in determining the success or otherwise of the final outcome. 'Certain forms of explanation are more effective at preventing a wrong decision,' Doshi-Velez says. It's something the Google Health researchers have noticed, too. In their field trial in Thailand, says Google product manager Lily Peng, a system notification that an image was ungradable and that there should be a referral could very easily be misinterpreted. 'For some people it means being referred to retinal specialists, which is at the higher end of care, versus refer for human review, which is what ended up being part of the protocol,' she explains.

'It's not just about the machine-learning part, it's about figuring out how to present the information as well,' Doshi-Velez argues, stressing the point that conclusions reached by an AI system need to make humans think. Such conclusions can't be too easy to accept or they risk becoming relied upon without that crucial element of critical thinking. By the same token, they can't be too hard to digest or humans will simply ignore or gloss over them. 'Models need to be transparent in their limitations, highlighting situations in which the AI prediction may not be accurate or valid,' the Harvard study concludes.

But when humans and AI are in sync, the potential benefits are huge. The more positive outcomes of the Harvard project, for example, suggest AI could eventually help with diagnosis for a mental health condition that is often missed and for which treatments vary wildly. They start to offer hope for the more than 264 million people around the world who battle with depression.

AI vs humans or AI with humans?

What, then, does the future hold for AI and the world of work in the medium term? It's likely to be a mixed bag of results. There have been and will continue to be disappointments and failures along the way. In 2018 IBM had to ditch a multi-million-dollar project designed to help the treatment of cancer patients after it was found to be giving clinicians bad advice.[62] During the coronavirus pandemic Walmart abandoned the use of robots to scan shelves and assess levels of stock when it realised humans were just as effective.[63] An October 2020 study conducted by the MIT Sloan Management Review and the Boston Consulting Group, which surveyed more than 3,000 business leaders running companies with annual revenues above $100 million, discovered that only in 10 per cent of cases did people feel that the investment they made in AI produced a 'significant' return.[64]

AI will cause disruption, too. 'Better-educated, better-paid workers will be the most affected by the new technology, with some exceptions,' research from the Brookings Institution found in November 2019. Those whose jobs currently involve a close focus on data will be particularly vulnerable: market researchers, sales managers, computer programmers and personal finance advisers among them. Those whose jobs involve a lot of interpersonal skills, such as those in education and social care, will probably be less affected: AI is very unlikely to replace human compassion and empathy. That said, in Japan care robots are already used to help the country's ageing population. And in any case, it's dangerous to make sweeping generalisations. The fact is that AI adoption will vary around the world according to local culture and social attitudes. Automation in finance in Singapore is likely to be very different from automation in finance in Pakistan.

If Google's work with computer vision or Harvard's study with psychiatrists are anything to go by, though, it seems likely that the general trend will be for AI not to replace existing jobs but to transform them – and to create new ones, too. Already, thousands of roles exist that would have been unimaginable at the turn of the century. Scores of people now work on AI labelling, helping to compile datasets that train machine learning. Thousands of individuals have been taken on at companies such as Facebook and YouTube to moderate content that might be breaking their platforms' rules, which has in many cases been initially flagged by an AI.

Researchers at MIT Sloan and Boston argue that those companies poised to benefit most from AI are those who use it to augment and shape traditional processes rather than replace them. In other words, they create an environment in which humans learn from AI and AI learns from humans. The toolmaker Stanley Black & Decker is one example. It has started using computer vision to check the quality of the tape measures it manufactures. The system flags defects in real time, spotting problems early in the production cycle and so reducing wastage. But humans are still on hand to inspect and make judgement calls on the worst faults.

Experts are key to creating trustworthy AI systems, says Ken Chatfield, the vice-president of research at Tractable, an AI firm that uses computer vision to help make decisions about insurance claims after car crashes – its AI is being used in the real world by some of the biggest insurance companies. The company initially trained its AI on thousands of images of vehicles that had been in accidents – involving damaged door panels, broken windscreens and more. But it saw the biggest improvements in the system's performance when the damage highlighted in images had been labelled by specialists, with years of experience in assessing crash reports. And it is human insurance agents who take over once the AI has reviewed images and suggested what the next steps should be. 'The data in itself is not enough, and also our knowledge as researchers is not enough – we really need to draw on the knowledge of experts in order to be able to train models,' Chatfield explains. 'Involving the expert is also what we need to build up trust'.

The London-based lawyer Richard Robinson, the CEO of Robin AI, has struck a not dissimilar balance in the legal field. He quit his job at a large law firm when he became convinced that many of the repetitive tasks that went into contract work could be automated. 'A lot of what I would spend my time doing as a lawyer felt like it didn't need much brain power,' he explains. His view was that machine learning could be utilised for reviewing some types of contract, such as those concerned with employment conditions. The tasks involved seemed simple enough.

It didn't, however, turn out that way. 'The truth is it was much more difficult than we anticipated,' Robinson says. 'There are so many random things that could be in that document, that you can't be confident that the AI will always identify them.' What he therefore did was to create a system in which AI works with human lawyers rather than instead of them. The company's system has been trained on historical contracts – both those in the public domain and documents provided by clients – and taught to look for particular elements. It's therefore able to detect whether a non-compete clause has been sneakily added into a business contract, or whether an employment contract stipulates non-standard working hours.

If it finds anomalies, the system alerts a human lawyer via email and they then check the document. The same thing happens if the system is unable to interpret a particular clause or contract. A recent assignment the company took on was checking contracts between big fast-food retailers and their suppliers during the early months of the coronavirus pandemic, to find out what each party's obligations were in the event of a crisis. Robinson's view is that lawyers find checking contracts tedious. At the same time, it's dangerous to rely wholly on AI, because even if it's getting things right 96 per cent of the time, that's not good enough when companies' and individuals' lives and livelihoods are at stake. 'We want to use AI to make the first attempt at everything in situations where it's really easy for a person to check and see if it's wrong or right,' he says.

However organisations end up using AI, there's no doubt that as it spreads it will become easier to access and operate. At present most AI deployments involve handcrafted technology. In the future, a company's AI requirements may be handled by a third party, using software that seems as straightforward as that inside word processors or slideshow builders. A company that wants to use AI to analyse specific datasets or images will be able to use a template to create this. The algorithm it picks may not have been created by the third-party service they're buying the template from, but from another company further up the chain of businesses developing and industrialising AI. The technology will become plug-and-play. By that point we may hardly notice its interaction with our daily lives.

Once this happens the world really will change significantly. People's workplaces will face automation at a greater scale than at any point so far this millennium. For many the entire nature of work may change. How we interact with businesses and government services will also be transformed. Societies that deploy AI will need to learn how people react to the technology and what their expectations of it are. At the same time, individuals will only follow the directions given by an AI if the system works efficiently, is understandable – and can be trusted.

6

Weaponising AI

AI's inexorable rise has been accompanied by its politi-
cisation. This is not just because it offers the potential
for societies to operate more efficiently, or that it is
now intricately bound up with their economic success.
It's because it's become a weapon in the struggle for a
technological dominance that carries with it immense
political power. In the 1960s the former Soviet Union
and the USA competed in the space race. Today it's the
USA and the growing superpower that is China that are
seeking supremacy in the struggle to achieve control of
the world of technology and its infrastructure.

The politics

For a long time, it has been Western universities, technology companies and policymakers that drive innovation,

with talent from around the world flocking to the US to work on AI. Now, China is seeking to drive forward tech standards in everything from 5G to AI developments. Its ambitions are serious. In 2017, the country's ruling Communist Party announced its aim to be world leader in AI by 2030. It's currently spending billions on AI development, much of it in the private sector. Analysis from the US think tank the Center for Security and Emerging Technology suggests that the Chinese government spent around the same amount on AI investment in 2018 as the US planned to in 2020.[65] Others have claimed that its expenditure is actually far outstripping that of the US.

Other metrics, too, show China's commitment. Since 2005 it has published more AI research papers than the US, even if they haven't all had the same impact on the academic community as US-based work. That, however, is set to change, according to analysis by the Allen Institute for AI in May 2019 which suggested that within a year the number of Chinese-led research papers cited by others would match the number of US ones being cited[66]

– although the Institute says this growth may be partly fuelled by a virtuous circle, where Chinese researchers may increasingly cite more Chinese researchers.

China may currently lag behind the US and other nations in its AI hardware development, but it nevertheless now boasts some of the world's leading AI software companies. SenseTime, Face++ and Hikvision are all prominent in facial recognition. Alibaba, Baidu and Tencent now rival Google, Facebook, Microsoft and Apple in their spending power and appeal to AI would-be employees.

And the country is spreading its influence across many of the world's less economically developed countries. China's Belt and Road scheme has provided developing nations with new technology that will in future become fuelled by AI. 'In Africa the backend network infrastructure is basically almost entirely Chinese now, between Huawei and ZTE,' says Eric Olander, who leads the China Africa Project. 'In Ghana, they've gone from 700 [CCTV] cameras to 7,000 cameras in the space of just a few years.' During the coronavirus pandemic, Olander adds, Chinese companies donated technology to African states to help them fight the virus. Huawei, for example, provided video conference systems and thermal temperature scanners, as well as some cash, during the spring of 2020.

Tech rivalry isn't limited to China and the US, though: other countries around the world are investing in AI research and development, aiming to keep up with the global leaders and seeking to deploy the technologies across their own nations. It's unlikely that such competition will lead to the fracturing of the technology, or into a simple two-way split between the US and China. Most of the world's AI development is far too interconnected to be completely driven apart by political rivalries. It's dominated by open-source publishing, research, breakthroughs and training datasets that are available to anyone with an internet connection. Nevertheless, international tensions are likely to increase as China aims to achieve its superpower targets.

In immediate terms the expansion of AI has raised questions of regulation. Some claim that existing laws, covering human rights and data protection, are sufficient to keep abuses in check. Others argue that AI raises wholly new issues that can only be dealt with by specific laws. Some are nervous about particular aspects of AI technology (several US cities have banned the use of facial-recognition technology). Some believe that it should not be used at all in certain domains (there is a wide consensus among the AI community that the technology should not be used for autonomous weapon systems, such as drones, that can take lives without human intervention).

The European Union may end up leading the way in such matters. Its General Data Protection Regulation (GDPR), whose enforcement began in 2018, has redefined the way people's personal information is handled around the world. Now it has now turned its attention to codifying laws on the use and control of AI, which, if and when issued, would constitute the first transnational regulation of AI (the guidelines were scheduled for publication in 2020, but then delayed to an unspecified date in 2021). 'We want a set of rules that puts people at the centre,' said Ursula von der Leyen, the European president, in September 2020. 'Algorithms must not be a black box, and there must be clear rules if something goes wrong.'

Von der Leyen's comments followed the publication of a white paper setting out what the EU might do: for example, introducing rules to govern 'high-risk' AI systems (such as those used in health, policing and transport) and those cases where AI use could result in discrimination or injury or put people's lives in danger. It's worth noting, though, that a consensus view is some way off. Of the more than 1,200 groups the EU consulted, 42 per cent thought that new laws were needed to govern AI, while 33 per cent argued that existing legislation could do the job. There was a similar split over possible approaches to high-risk uses of AI (42 per cent to 30 per cent). Clearly there is a long way to go.

The hackers

If countries are in the process of using AI as a tool reinforcing power and dominance, criminals are also starting to weaponise the technology. First among them will be hacker and cybercriminal communities.

The problem is that it currently doesn't take much to fool an AI. Simply adding strips of black and white tape to red stop signs (in some cases spelling out the words 'love' and 'hate') – as a group of nine researchers did in 2018 in a virtual simulation – can be sufficient to fool a self-driving car into assuming that the speed limit is 45 miles per hour.[67] Neural networks have been tricked into misinterpreting a picture of a turtle as a rifle,[68] a panda as a gibbon,[69] a school bus as an ostrich,[70] and a coffee pot as a macaw.[71] A particular pattern applied to the frame of a pair of glasses has proved sufficient to cause facial recognition software to make an incorrect identification.[72]

These errors occurred in research conditions. But cybercriminals and hackers always work at the cutting edges of technology and innovation – it's the only way to stay in front of law enforcement officials. It won't be long before they turn to using AI. For some AI will be the tool rather than the target. For instance, criminals may use AI to help find flaws in an app's code (app developers also do this to pre-emptively find errors). They may employ AI to create new malware or attacks (polymorphic malware can constantly change itself to evade detection). Or they may program AI to mimic people's behaviour as part of phishing attacks that con people into believing an email or request for money is being sent from someone they trust.

In some respects, the cybersecurity industry is ahead of criminals, as it has long been using AI tools that can detect anomalies, such as malware, in a corporate network that could cause extensive damage to data and systems. Google, for example, started using machine learning in 2017 to help spot malicious Android apps in its PlayStore. Emily Wenger from the University of Chicago's SAND Lab, along with other researchers, used AI to create a privacy-preserving tool, Fawkes, that adds data to people's photos in a process called image cloaking. This added data is invisible to the human eye but can confuse facial recognition databases.[73] 'The idea is that if you post these cloaked photos online and someone scrapes them and tries to use them to train an unauthorised facial recognition model, that model will learn this bogus representation of you,' Wenger says. But criminals and malicious actors have the incentive – and the tools – to catch up.

As well as using AI to attack conventional computer systems, AI can be employed to attack other AI. The risks and stakes here are high, and malicious uses of the technology are hard to detect. Essentially it can take one of two forms: adversarial attacks and Trojan attacks. With an adversarial attack 'perturbations' – or pixels that aren't visible to the human eye – are added to an image to make the AI misinterpret what it is seeing. (This uses GAN-style technology, which was first created by Google researchers in 2014 when they published a paper that described how adding a 'perturbation' to an image made it perform incorrectly.[74]) 'Perturbations' are, effectively, a more sophisticated version of the stop sign phenomenon described above. As Dawn Song, a professor of computer science at the University of California, Berkeley, who was involved with the street sign manipulation project, told *WIRED* in 2018: 'Adversarial examples are just illustrating that we still just have very limited understanding of how deep learning works and their limitations.'[75]

Trojan attacks, by contrast, involve planting malicious data in one piece of AI that might well end up being used by a different one. So, for example, a company might purchase an image-recognition system from another firm that deals with the training and creation of AI, not knowing that it has already been hacked. Only when they – or an end user even further down the supply chain – deploy it will the problems surface. 'You'll probably have a bunch of test data yourself,' says Wenchao Li, an assistant professor at Boston University who has exposed how Trojan attacks can impact reinforcement-learning algorithms.

'You've tested the model and it seems right on this test dataset. And now you can deploy it. But the problem is, the network that you got from somebody else actually has a Trojan in it.'

Such systemic threats have been a part of the digital world for years. The laptop, computer and phone manufacturer ASUS, for example, suffered a supply chain attack in 2019 after a server for the company's software updates was compromised and malware inserted into the legitimate update that was sent out.[76] About 500,000 devices were hit by the malicious update, which went unnoticed in ASUS's updates for around five months. AI Trojan horses are more complex. That, however, doesn't make them any less feasible.

To help combat such backdoor attacks against AI systems the US Intelligence Advanced Research Projects Activity (IARPA) has come up with a project called TrojAI whereby researchers compete to find effective methods to detect Trojans. 'For a Trojan attack to be effective the trigger must be rare in the normal operating environment, so that the Trojan does not activate on test datasets or in normal operations, either one of which could raise the suspicions of the AI's users,' IARPA says on its website.[77] Those working on the project have to try to detect an AI system that has a Trojan installed, without having any access to its training data or the underlying mechanisms behind the AI.

Detecting these types of attacks is difficult. 'There's an argument for an attacker to poison only a tiny fraction of the data, because, let's say, this one bad player needed a team, and you could have a vigilant vendor monitoring the training process,' says Boston's Li, who is part of one of the teams in the IARPA project.

At present, the TrojAI project is in its early stages, but those behind it say it shows promise. However, inspecting for a Trojan involves deep analysis of the results of an AI system, and being able to undertake this requires another AI that's able to carefully classify many different outputs of the corrupted system and spot how it reaches its decisions. Such complexity inevitably gives potential hackers room for manoeuvre. The battle between legitimate AI users and hackers will be a continual one.

7

Making AI accountable

Silicon Valley's biggest technology companies – Google, Amazon, Facebook, Netflix, Microsoft and Apple – have driven the development and commercialisation of AI throughout the 2010s. They have invested billions to build the infrastructure required to process AI decisions and then deploy AI in their products. They have invested heavily in securing the vast amount of data their AI systems are trained on, processing it in huge data centres and deploying immense computing power to crunch it. And they have spent a small fortune on attracting and keeping the best possible talent.

Thanks to them our lives have been quietly transformed. Amazon has brought voice-recognition technology into millions of homes with its Alexa-enabled Echo speakers. Apple has pioneered privacy-protecting machine learning which strips away personal details from your interactions with your phone, to ensure people can't be re-identified from the training data it supplies. Microsoft's tech infrastructure sits behind hundreds of other companies' AI systems. Facebook and Instagram feeds are filled with the posts that AI decides we're most likely to interact with, not just from our friends and family but also advertisers and brands that people follow. Netflix's machine learning nudges us towards the shows and movies it wants us to watch, based on our past viewing history. The vast majority of Google's products – including suggested replies in emails and documents, its translation tools, directions provided by maps and YouTube recommendations – are fuelled by AI.

But there's a problem. The vast majority of AI products are being developed by one particular group: white men. Just as decisions made by AI can be skewed by the datasets that feed them, their basic creation can be skewed by the cultural background and assumptions of those who build it. 'What really matters at the end of the day is who is building and shaping the AI system,' says Tess Posner, the CEO of non-profit AI4ALL. 'Who really is in a position of power to influence what gets built, what's designed, what's created? Right now, that's a very homogenous group of technologists. You can only know so much if you're a group of individuals who represent one type of person and background.'

Ironically for a sector that is so heavily reliant on data, the world of AI is remarkably coy when it comes to revealing data about the nature of its workforce. Technology companies, universities and other academic institutions alike have traditionally been reluctant to publish details. Things are slowly changing for large companies in some countries, but they're still able to control the narrative that accompanies the statistics they issue. Overall, there's a distinct lack of detail about such metrics as gender, sexual orientation or ethnicity.

Even so, the general picture is clear. On average 80 per cent of AI professors are male, according to the 2018 AI Index, which looked at such top computer science schools as University College London, Stanford, CMU, Berkeley, Oxford, ETH Zurich and the University of Illinois' Urbana-Champaign campus (the researchers noted that there was 'little variation' between the schools inspected).[78] Research from Nesta[79] and the World Economic Forum (WEF)[80] suggests that the proportion of academic AI papers co-authored by at least one woman 'has not improved since the 1990s' (analysis by WEF shows Germany, Brazil, Mexico and Argentina to have the largest gender gaps). Only 2.5 per cent of Google's workforce is black, while for Facebook and Microsoft it's 4 per cent – and those percentages are total ones: there is little or no data available for roles that are specifically concerned with AI, or that offers a detailed breakdown of the minorities involved.[81]

Not surprisingly, a 2019 report on gender, race and power in AI from New York University's AI Now Institute that discussed these numbers concludes that 'The AI industry is strikingly homogeneous, due in large part to its treatment of women, people of colour, gender minorities, and other under-represented groups.'[82] It continues: 'The AI industry needs to make significant structural changes to address systemic racism, misogyny, and lack of diversity.' DeepMind researchers Shakir Mohamed, Marie-Therese Png and William Isaac view the problem in colonial terms.[83] 'Any commitment to building the responsible and beneficial AI of the future ties us to the hierarchies, philosophy and technology inherited from the past, and a renewed responsibility to the technology of the present,' the trio write.

The colonial nature of AI takes various forms. It's embedded in its algorithmic discrimination, which allows an unequal real world to be reflected in an unequal virtual one. It runs through the sector's hiring practices. It involves the widespread use of low-paid labour in relatively poor parts of the world among those at the beginning of the AI production chain who prepare data for training. People benefit financially from the jobs they do, of course, but it's questionable whether their communities are likely to benefit from the technologies they're helping to create. And then there's the fact that AI governance rules tend to be set by richer countries. Mohamed, Png and Isaac highlight a global review of AI ethics guidelines that found Africa, South and Central America and Central Asia to be absent from discussions. They also point out that AI systems can be beta-tested in countries where data protection laws aren't as strong as they are in, say, the UK or Europe.

Such systemic injustices are manifested in individual experiences: people who have been under-paid for the job they do, or not received the job promotion they deserved, or been treated disrespectfully by colleagues. Recent years have seen thousands of Google employees protest at their companies' handling of sexual harassment allegations against senior executives and failing to properly investigate discrimination claims, in addition to hundreds of Microsoft employees claiming they had been victim to harassment and discrimination while at work. In December 2020, leading AI ethics researcher Timnit Gebru said Google fired her and accused the company of being 'institutionally racist' after it took issue with an academic paper she co-authored.[84] More than 6,000 AI people, including several thousand Google staff, signed an open letter supporting Gebru.[85] In response Google CEO Sundar Pichai apologised for the controversy and said the company needed to 'accept responsibility for the fact that a prominent black, female leader with immense talent left Google unhappily'.[86] Consistent failings at the heart of AI development reinforce the argument that to have a chance of working for everybody, the technology needs to be built and controlled by a diverse and representative set of people.

'Diverse' and 'representative' means also taking account of the more than one billion people around the world who live with disabilities. AI has helped create new forms of accessibility – for example, computer vision apps that can 'see' for people. But there is a long way to go to before it's truly inclusive. 'I think the most important step in inclusive AI is involving people with disabilities at all stages,' says Mary Bellard, the principal innovation architect and AI for Accessibility program lead at

Microsoft. Such inclusion involves more than testing products on people with disabilities. It has to include hiring technologists with disabilities, too. 'Sometimes there is this concept of building technology "for people with disabilities", instead of "with or by people with disabilities", and there is an important distinction between those two ideas,' Bellard says.

But there are people and organisations around that are trying to change things. One such is Tess Posner's AI4ALL, the US non-profit set-up that is seeking to get more young women and BAME people interested in AI. Among its initiatives are summer camps for high-school students. 'We hear a lot of things like, "I'm the only person at my school who looks like me who's interested in this," or "I never thought I can go into this field because I don't see anyone like me in the field,"' says Posner. The summer camps are designed to introduce such students to AI role models. PhD students and experts from big technology firms explain the main principles of AI: the types of machine learning, how to use the programming language Python, the importance of datasets within AI. AI4ALL also provides open-sourced AI teaching resources to high-school teachers around the US, targeting them at lower-income schools, which may not typically have the money to invest in computer science-specific education for their students. Posner aims to get the teaching resources translated into other languages so they can be disseminated more widely both within and outside the US.

AI Now's diversity report looks at ways in which the technology industry in general and AI in particular can make changes. It argues for the publication of pay levels, including bonuses and all other payments, across all roles and jobs, broken down by race and gender. It pushes for pay equality to be established to ensure people are being properly compensated for the work they're doing, and for the promotion of currently under-represented groups to be built into company targets. It also demands that harassment and discrimination transparency reports should be published. Perhaps most crucially, it campaigns for a shake-up in the way people are recruited, suggesting that initiatives should be set up to reach out to non-elite universities, and that better ways should be found to allow contractors, temporary staff and freelancers to become full-time employees. Hiring practices and conditions should also be made transparent, so that everyone knows how individuals are hired, paid and promoted. Responsibility for all this begins with senior management. 'Those at the top of corporate hierarchies have much more power to set direction and shape ethical decision-making than do individual researchers and developers,' says AI Now's report.

Transparency and regulation

Joy Buolamwini has shown accountability in AI can lead to change. In 2015 the graduate student of MIT's Media Lab was sitting at her laptop, trying to get the generic face-tracking software she was using to work. The problem was that it wouldn't. It was supposed to project digital artwork onto her face, but it couldn't 'see' her.

When, however, her friend sat in front of the cheap laptop webcam the system automatically sprang to life. The reason? Buolamwini is black. Her friend is white. Once Buolamwini donned a white mask, the software instantly spotted her.

This wasn't the first time Buolamwini had encountered the discrimination arising from algorithms trained mostly on images of people with white skin. She had once tried to teach a robot how to play peek-a-boo. It didn't respond. Again, she was invisible.

Five years after Buolamwini sat in front of her webcam, her research has changed how facial-recognition technologies are developed, and brought the issue of selection bias in training data to general awareness. Her 2018 MIT thesis, 'Gender Shades', which was co-authored by Timnit Gebru, audited the performance of facial-recognition systems from IBM, Microsoft and Chinese firm Face++, and offered a stark wake-up call.[87]

What she showed was that, overall, the systems were worse at recognising people with darker skin than they were at recognising those with lighter skin. Microsoft performed best, but even so, its 87.1 per cent accuracy for darker-skinned people compared poorly with its 99.3 per cent accuracy for lighter-skinned subjects. The margin of difference in IBM's software was 19.2 per cent. And when gender was introduced, accuracy rates dropped further. Both IBM and Face++ recognised darker-skinned females correctly only 65 per cent of the time. Microsoft was slightly better at 79 per cent. For lighter-skinned females all three sets of software scored above 92 per cent. The differences in performance were as high as 34 per cent.

Follow-up research a year later – called 'Actionable Auditing'[88] – from Buolamwini and Inioluwa Deborah Raji claimed to find similar problems with Amazon's facial-recognition technology (the company disputed this). But by this time IBM, Microsoft and Face++ had all improved their algorithms. IBM's error difference dropped from 34.4 per cent to 16.71 per cent; Microsoft's from 20.8 per cent to 1.52 per cent; and Face++'s from 33.7 per cent to 3.6 per cent. 'The study was able to motivate companies to prioritise the issue and yield significant improvements within months,' wrote Buolamwini and Raji.

By holding opaque algorithms and their creators to account, the hugely influential 'Gender Shades' and follow-up study have shown a way forward. They have very publicly exposed the failures of existing AI systems and led to a much-needed public debate, not just about how facial-recognition systems operate, but about how they should be used. Buolamwini has appeared before legislators, policymakers and police officials to explain how the discriminatory practices worked, and how her audits uncovered them. Her work has directly contributed to greater scrutiny of facial-recognition systems. It's also led to them being banned in a number of US states. In June 2020, Amazon, IBM and Microsoft all committed, at least temporarily, to stop selling facial-recognition software to police, following global protests about systematic racism and the killing of George Floyd at the hands of Minneapolis police.

The ripples of the pioneering work done by Buolam-wini and others will spread out over the next few years, as lawmakers and regulators all grapple with the issues that AI throws up. In particular, there will need to be a recognition that constant structured auditing, of the type that Buolamwini undertook, is essential. Not only does it lead to better systems, but it also forces people to address how those systems are utilised and if they should be used at all.

At present, uncertainty about the application of AI is very widespread. 'Currently we cannot say which local authorities in the UK, for instance, are using an algorithmic decision system to inform prioritisation in children's social care,' says Jenny Brennan, an AI policy researcher and software engineer at the Ada Lovelace Institute. 'What is really clear is that we do need ways for regulators to inspect algorithmic systems.' The same uncertainty and need for inspection exists across other sectors in which AI is utilised, not just in the UK but across the world.

In Amsterdam and Helsinki city authorities have started tackling a lack of transparency by introducing registers for AI used by city departments, says Linda van de Fliert, the programme manager for Amsterdam's algorithm register.[89] The system, which at the time of writing contains just four AI examples operating in fields such as property rental and automated parking controls, seeks to capture the AI via descriptions of the system's architecture and its datasets. If the AI is developed by a third-party company, they are contractually bound to provide details for the purposes of openness and transparency. Over the coming years, van de Fliert says, non-AI algorithms, such as the simple ones used in spreadsheets, will be added. 'The register is about trust. Journalists can go to the register, activists can go to the register, and they can look at what the city is doing.'

For her part, Jenny Brennan pinpoints two approaches for assessing AI systems that are either currently in use or being considered. One is an algorithm audit that includes a bias audit and regulatory inspections. The other is an algorithmic impact assessment, which might include considering the societal impact of an AI before or after it is in use. Her research concludes, though, that there is some way to go before it's clear precisely what the best versions of these systems would look like in practice.

'There's a lack of clarity around when algorithmic decisions are being used, and there's usually not a way for folks to actually compare notes and see if there is evidence of bias or any of those sorts of issues,' says Alice Xiang, the head of fairness, transparency and accountability research at the Partnership on AI. The organisation is a research body that is backed by more than 100 groups, including Apple, Amazon, Google, Microsoft, Samsung and IBM. 'There's a lot of constraints in terms of the proprietary nature of the data used to train algorithms and also the proprietary nature of the algorithms themselves.'

The current opaqueness of AI decisions makes it harder for people to oppose them, Xiang says. True, there was a prominent backlash against Apple's credit card launch in the US when its algorithms appeared to show bias by offering different credit limits to men and women, but such a reaction is rare. 'When you have, say, millions of users being affected, even if just a small cluster of folks got together and managed to talk to each other and compare notes, that's not necessarily really great evidence to go forth with a lawsuit, and even that rarely happens.'

There is disagreement as to who should be responsible for audits and assessments. Dozens of AI ethics groups and guidelines have been drawn up, but many of them lack real power. (In one rare pro-active instance in August 2020, a UK police ethics board stopped the development and deployment of flawed AI that was supposed to predict if someone would commit violent crime.[90]) Some AI experts believe existing regulators, such as those that handle financial laws or education bodies, should be responsible for inspecting the AI that falls within the ambit of their current expertise. Others believe entirely new bodies should be set up. In practice, a mix of approaches seems the most likely.

In July 2020 the government of New Zealand launched a set of standards that it called an algorithmic charter and a 'world first'.[91] Twenty-one government agencies pledged to be transparent about how they use algorithms in decision-making. They undertook to give 'plain English' explanations of how systems worked, and promised to make efforts to manage any biases that might be informing them. In addition, the charter stipulates that algorithmic decision-making systems should be regularly peer-reviewed, that humans should retain oversight of the systems, and that there should be public access to government agencies deploying them. Agencies must also consider the views of Te Ao Māori, or Indigenous people, on data collection, and consult with people whose lives are affected by the algorithms.

'There are so many sources of bias: individuals, structural, societal, it seems dangerous and a bit arrogant to think that we can fix all this with one system,' argues Suresh Venkatasubramanian, a professor in the School of Computing at the University of Utah. He says that each of the potential risks a system poses should be identified, and that it should be audited for them one at a time. 'The goal is to narrow the scope of the harms to the point where we can actually deliver an audit that makes sense for that,' he explains, 'and then slowly try to build up from there.' Audits have to be done at the right stage of the development process, too. 'Often the use of audit risk compliance teams are the last people anybody calls,' says Rumman Chowdhury, the former head of Accenture Applied Intelligence's Responsible AI division, who left to create the algorithmic audit company Parity. 'Ethical assessment is not something you can just do once. There are certain actions you would take at different stages. It wouldn't even be appropriate to do, for example, a data audit at the very end of product development.' Crucially, any audit has to evolve over time, as new problematic issues are identified or if the training data or algorithms used in the AI application change.

In the absence of widespread legislation and auditing that can expose threats, discrimination and biases in AI systems being used around the world, Buolamwini's non-profit Algorithmic Justice League is taking measures into its own hands. In the world of cybersecurity ethical hackers that report flaws or vulnerabilities in software can be paid for their work through bug bounty systems. The Algorithmic Justice League is learning from this process by running an algorithmic vulnerability bounty project – people can disclose how they have been treated by AI and it will be investigated. Ultimately, Buolamwini believes that to develop AI that can be a benefit to all, everyone has to be involved in its creation. 'It's so easy to think you might introduce technology to solve other people's problems without actually bringing the people who are most impacted into the community. So [it's] not designing for but designing with.'[92]

8
The future of AI

AI is now firmly embedded as an integral part of our everyday lives. Over the coming decades it will become more powerful and more sophisticated. It will go from being used widely on social networks and in tech products to being used by businesses and within society.

But what about the ultimate goal of some researchers: AGI, or artificial general intelligence? AGI would represent a revolutionary step forward. At the moment AI is proving better than humans at some specific tasks but, depending on which definition you use, AGI would be able to perform excellently at every task that it is given. It could, to all intents and purposes, have fully human capabilities.

For some, this would be the nightmare scenario. Elon Musk, the founder, co-founder or CEO of SpaceX, Tesla and Neuralink, who has frequently had run-ins with the

AI community for his outspoken views on AGI and other forms of super-intelligence, argues that AGI would be more dangerous than nuclear weapons, and that the technology is a 'fundamental risk to the existence of human civilisation'. He has warned of AI networks developing their own consciousness, as rapid automation happens. 'You say, "What harm can a deep intelligence in the network do?" Well, it can start a war by doing fake news and spoofing email accounts and doing fake press releases and by manipulating information,' he said in 2017.[93]

He is not alone. The philosopher Nick Bostrom, the head of Oxford University's Future of Humanity Institute, has repeatedly warned that creating super-intelligence could lead to the 'extinction of mankind'. In March 2015, Bostrom, Musk, the co-founders of DeepMind, Stephen Hawking, and AI leaders from Google, Facebook and hundreds of other institutions signed an open letter stating that if general intelligence is the ultimate goal, safety measures need to be put in place to ensure that it benefits and does not harm society.[94]

In 2018, researchers at the Australian National University set out to chart how the risks of AGI could be mitigated.[95] The problem they faced was that no one really knows what AGI might look like. 'We can only guess at the technology, algorithms, and structure that will be used,' the researchers wrote. 'Indeed, even if we had the blueprint of an AGI system, understanding and predicting its behaviour might still be hard.' José Hernández-Orallo, an AI professor at the Universitat Politècnica de València who is also a principal investigator on a University of Cambridge project analysing the risk of AGI, takes a more sceptical view. 'There might be a moment that we get systems that are able to learn skills faster and better than humans and a wider range of skills,' he explains. 'And that will be AGI, and we can say that these are superhuman in all ways. But I don't think we will decide to build them in the short term.'

Hernández-Orallo's prognosis is that we will reach a middle ground between AI and 'complete' AGI where systems exist that possess much greater knowledge than people do for a wide range of tasks, but don't know everything. To solve new problems, they will require more data which will have to be obtained by their human owners. 'To me, AGI is a system that has a general ability, which means that it can learn any possible skill, some of them easier than others, as happens with us,' he says. 'That doesn't mean that the system is superintelligent. But that's going to be transformative.'

Whatever form of AGI is ultimately achieved, practical and ethical questions arise. How safe will it be to rely on the decisions made by AGI, given that we won't understand by what steps it arrived at those decisions? How do we decide when to employ AGI and when to rely on humans? 'There are thousands of clever people working in AI research. They can probably carry out their research and development without a definition of AGI,' says Ragnar Fjelland, a professor at the University of Bergen.

What they should keep in mind, however, is not just the question of what computers can do, but also the question of what computers should do.

This question includes ethical considerations. Sometimes it is right to replace humans by technology. However, the basic attitude should be that technology should improve the human condition, and not replace humans.

One point most AI researchers do agree on is that if AGI is ever created, it won't be for a very long time. Of the 352 machine-learning researchers asked in a 2017 survey when they believed human-level machine intelligence could be achieved, a mean of 50 per cent gave the chance of the milestone being achieved as being 45 years away.[96] On aggregate, researchers from Asia predicted human-level performance would be achieved in 30 years, while those from North America predicted 74 years. The average date given by 23 leading AI experts for a 50 per cent chance of AGI is 2099, according to the futurist Martin Ford in his book *Architects of Intelligence.*[97] Interestingly most of the participants were unwilling for their names to appear alongside their predictions.

Such unwillingness to put one's reputation on the line is hardly surprising when something as vague as AGI is involved. If nobody can agree what it is, then it's impossible to know what tools will be needed to create it and whether they already exist or will need to be invented. If more technological breakthroughs are required – as seems likely – there's no guessing when these might occur. And even if some form of AGI is achieved, people will doubtless disagree whether what has been created really is AGI. When Google claimed in 2019 that it had achieved quantum supremacy – the ability to use a computer operating according to the principles of quantum mechanics to complete a task faster than a traditional computer – its rival IBM contested its results and argued that quantum supremacy doesn't really matter anyway.[98] The same could occur with AGI. 'I think that with the way some [AI] breakthroughs are presented, they come with more fuss and more overhype than they used to,' warns José Hernández-Orallo. He adds that researchers and tech firms need to be 'very careful' with how they present AI research.

The AI systems we already have are far from mastering their current learning approaches, and are not able to perform tasks that are different from the one they are trained on. There's a long way to go before humans will achieve an AI that's general and that can work across many different domains.

But there's still plenty of progress to be made with the technology we currently have. AI is already transforming and disrupting the world around us. It's throwing up all sorts of challenges. There are ethical, societal and technical issues that need fixing with the systems we have right now. Those building AI need to take responsibility for their creations. They need to ask whether the systems they are making are improving the world around us and if they are likely to be abused by those with malicious intents. They should speak to the people their technology impacts and understand what difference it makes. The deployment of AI needs to work for everyone. The pursuit of AGI shouldn't distract from that.

Glossary

AGI (artificial general intelligence)

An AI system that can think like a person, learn new tasks and understand the world as a human does. General intelligence is the goal of much AI research.

Computer vision

A computer's ability to 'see' via image recognition, object detection and classification, or object tracking. Computer vision can be used to process photos, recorded video and real-time footage.

CPU (central processing unit)

A computer chip that makes the calculations that tell a device how to operate. Containing billions of transistors, CPUs are adept at running some AI algorithms.

Deep learning

The subset of machine learning that uses multiple layers of neural networks to learn from data. Deep learning has been the biggest accelerator of AI use since the turn of the twenty-first century.

GAN (generative adversarial network)

AI that uses both supervised and unsupervised learning to generate new data based on previous data it has seen. The process has been used to create fake faces and produce AI-generated artwork.

GPU (graphics processing unit)

A graphics chip, originally developed for gaming, that has become favoured in AI as it has greater processing power than a CPU and so can speed up the training process. It's particularly useful for image recognition.

Neural network

A network, loosely modelled on the make-up of the brain, which facilitates machine learning. Calculations and predictions are made within each layer of the network.

NLP (natural language processing)

A way for computers to understand and use human language. This can include machine translation between languages, document summaries, speech-to-text conversion (and vice versa), and sentiment analysis.

Reinforcement learning

An algorithm that is given a clear goal – for instance, winning at a game – which it then attempts to reach through trial and error. Each time it does something that works it's rewarded; when it fails it may be penalised.

Supervised learning

The most common type of AI process. A supervised learning system makes predictions about information it hasn't seen before. To make those predictions, it is first shown previous examples of the problem it is trying to solve. Supervised learning is often used for image-recognition tasks.

Unsupervised learning

A learning system that looks for patterns in data that it has no previous knowledge of. Unlike supervised learning, unsupervised learning does not involve training with previous examples. It is useful for finding structure and classifying large amounts of data.

Acknowledgements

Anything created in this world isn't the product of one person – this book is no exception. While I have covered the growth of artificial intelligence – from its use within everything from healthcare to cybersecurity – at WIRED for more than five years, my knowledge of the decades-old industry still only scratches the surface. I am indebted to the expertise of others for the production of this book.

During my time at WIRED, the use of AI has grown exponentially and it now it seems as though society is at a true tipping point. The technology has crept into mainstream, daily use and will increasingly be set to work tackling new tasks in more areas of our lives. The promise of AI is hugely exciting: it has the potential to upend many of our daily activities and unlock new secrets about our planet (and beyond). It's not at all inconceivable to imagine AI reshaping the world as we know it. Despite this promise, there is still a lot of work to be done. We need to make sure the use of AI is fair, responsible and inclusive. Nobody should suffer because of the use of an AI system.

Thankfully, there are many immensely gifted and brilliant people working on the development of AI – both on ways to improve the world and making sure that AI works for everyone. During the course of reporting for this book many of these people spared their time and shared their deep expertise with me and I am truly grateful to them for doing this (particularly those who, during the height of coronavirus lockdown restrictions, put up with an interviewing technique that involved my sitting on my bedroom floor during a Zoom call).

Many of the people who contributed to the publication of this book are named and mentioned within its pages (although I won't hesitate, or apologise, before I list their names again here). However, there are others who played an equally important role who are not explicitly mentioned. In no particular order, I wish to pay thanks to: Adrian Weller, Alastair Moore, Alex Harvey, Alexander Babuta,

ACKNOWLEDGEMENTS

Alice Xiang, Bonaventure Dossou, Camille Marini, Chelsea Finn, Cori Crider, Daniel Leufer, David Dao, Emma Beede, Emily Wenger, Eric Olander, Fanny Hidvégi, Finale Doshi-Velez, Henry Ajder, Henry Shevlin, Jack Weast, Jeff Alstott, Jenny Brennan, José Hernández-Orallo, Julia Kreutzer, Jutta Treviranus, Kaiton Williams, Kanta Dihal, Ken Chatfield, Mark Harman, Mona Flores, Moshe Greenshpan, Nigel Toon, Lily Peng, Oren Etzioni, Ott Velsberg, Paul Newman, Ragnar Fjelland, Rashida Richardson, Renée Cummings, Richard Robinson, Rumman Chowdhury, Sandra Wachter, Sasha Luccioni, Saurabh Mishra, Shreya Shankar, Solon Barocas, Silvia Chiappa, Steven Feldstein, Suresh Venkatasubramanian, Tess Posner, Toshie Takahashi, Carol Reiley, Victor Riparbelli Rasmussen, Wenchao Li and William Isaac. The writing and reporting of Dave Gershgorn, Jack Clark, James Vincent, Karen Hao and Will Knight has set the agenda in the world of AI and is irreplaceable.

I also wish to thank all of the editorial team at WIRED for their continued support, particularly Greg Williams and Mike Dent for developing this series of books along with the team at Penguin. Much credit should go to Penguin's Nigel Wilcockson, who showed immeasurable patience and structural expertise throughout the many drafts of the manuscript. Rumman Chowdhury, the CEO of Parity AI, provided guidance on some areas of the book. Finally, but by no means least, I would not have been able to get through the pandemic-filled year and produce this book without the unwavering support of my partner, Stephanie. Her support and encouragement have made the entire thing possible.

This book is intended as an informed introduction to the world of AI and some of the opportunities and challenges the field presents. However, there is not enough space within these pages to explore some of the subjects with the depth they merit. Despite the time and expertise given by all those above – and countless others who are not named and came before them – any mistakes are my own. I hope that the book presents societal concerns with the gravity that they are intended and can, even in a tiny way, lead to the creation of a better AI future.

Notes

Notes to 1 The early years   pages 7–26

1   http://jmc.stanford.edu/articles/dartmouth/dartmouth.pdf

2   http://www-formal.stanford.edu/jmc/slides/dartmouth/
dartmouth/node1.html

3   https://www.nytimes.com/1958/07/13/archives/electronic-
brain-teaches-itself.html

4   https://cs.stanford.edu/people/eroberts/courses/soco/
projects/neural-networks/History/history1.html

5   https://hbr.org/1988/03/putting-expert-systems-to-work

6   http://www.chilton-computing.org.uk/inf/literature/
reports/lighthill_report/p001.htm

7   https://ai.stanford.edu/~nilsson/QAI/qai.pdf

8   https://www.nytimes.com/1997/05/12/nyregion/swift-and-
slashing-computer-topples-kasparov.html

9   https://arxiv.org/pdf/0706.3639.pdf

10   https://arxiv.org/pdf/0712.3329.pdf

Notes to 2 AI takes off   pages 27–42

11   https://www.nytimes.com/2012/06/26/technology/in-a-big-
     network-of-computers-evidence-of-machine-learning.html

12   https://arxiv.org/pdf/1112.6209.pdf

13   https://papers.nips.cc/paper/2012/file/
     c399862d3b9d6b76c8436e924a68c45b-Paper.pdf

14   https://www.wired.co.uk/article/deepmind

15   https://www.wired.com/2016/03/sadness-beauty-
     watching-googles-ai-play-go/

16   https://deepmind.com/blog/article/alphafold-a-solution-
     to-a-50-year-old-grand-challenge-in-biology

17   https://www.nature.com/articles/d41586-020-03348-4

18   https://en.yna.co.kr/view/AEN20191127004800315

19   https://www.rt.com/news/401731-ai-rule-world-putin/

20   https://hai.stanford.edu/research/ai-index-2019

21   https://www.stateofai2019.com/

Notes to 3 Applying AI   pages 43–73

22   https://news.mit.edu/2019/using-ai-predict-breast-cancer-
     and-personalize-care-0507

23 https://www.nature.com/articles/s41591-018-0107-6

24 https://www.wired.co.uk/article/deepmind-moorfields-ai-eye-nhs

25 https://www.thelancet.com/action/showPdf?pii =S2589-7500(19)30123-2

26 https://twitter.com/an_open_mind/status/ 1284487376312709120

27 https://arxiv.org/pdf/2005.14165.pdf

28 https://arxiv.org/pdf/1907.10597.pdf

29 https://arxiv.org/pdf/1906.02243.pdf

30 https://www.ntsb.gov/news/press-releases/Pages/ NR20200319.aspx

31 https://www.ntsb.gov/news/press-releases/Pages/ NR20200225.aspx

32 https://storage.googleapis.com/sdc-prod/v1/safety-report/ Waymo-Public-Road-Safety-Performance-Data.pdf

Notes to 4 AI's pitfalls   pages 75–107

33 https://www.propublica.org/article/machine-bias-risk-assessments-in-criminal-sentencing

34   http://epubs.surrey.ac.uk/852008/1/Biased%20
     Algorithm%20re%20Hispanics.pdf

35   https://papers.ssrn.com/sol3/papers.cfm?abstract_
     id=3333423

36   https://www.vice.com/en/article/5dpmdd/the-netherlands-
     is-becoming-a-predictive-policing-hot-spot

37   https://a27e0481-a3d0-44b8-8142-1376cfbb6e32.filesusr
     .com/ugd/b2dd23_21f6fe20f1b84c179abf440d4c049219.pdf

38   https://docs.google.com/forms/d/e/1FAIpQLSfdmQGrgdCB
     CexTrpne7KXUzpbiI9LeEtd0Am-qRFimpwuv1A/viewform

39   https://pubmed.ncbi.nlm.nih.gov/31649194/

40   https://www.hud.gov/sites/dfiles/Main/documents/HUD_v_
     Facebook.pdf

41   https://papers.ssrn.com/sol3/papers.cfm?abstract_
     id=3248829

42   https://www.nytimes.com/2020/06/24/technology/facial-
     recognition-arrest.html

43   https://www.vice.com/en/article/bv8k8a/faulty-facial-
     recognition-led-to-his-arrestnow-hes-suing

44 https://48ba3m4eh2bf2sksp43rq8kk-wpengine.netdna-ssl
    .com/wp-content/uploads/2019/07/London-Met-Police-
    Trial-of-Facial-Recognition-Tech-Report.pdf

45 https://carnegieendowment.org/2019/09/17/global-
    expansion-of-ai-surveillance-pub-79847

46 https://naiq.github.io/LTCC_Perosn_ReID.html

47 https://techcrunch.com/2020/03/11/india-used-facial-
    recognition-tech-to-identify-1100-individuals-at-a-recent-riot/

48 https://arxiv.org/pdf/2006.15873.pdf

49 https://www.nytimes.com/2019/04/14/technology/china-
    surveillance-artificial-intelligence-racial-profiling.html

50 https://sensity.ai/reports/

51 https://www.wired.co.uk/article/deepfake-porn-websites-
    videos-law

52 https://www.wired.co.uk/article/telegram-deepfakes-
    deepnude-ai

53 https://twitter.com/sensityai/status/1208451141350113284

54 https://about.fb.com/wp-content/uploads/2020/09/
    August-2020-CIB-Report.pdf

55   https://www.nisos.com/white-papers/rise_synthetic_
       audio_deepfakes

56   https://liamp.substack.com/p/my-gpt-3-blog-got-26-
       thousand-visitors

57   https://www.motherjones.com/politics/2019/03/deepfake-
       gabon-ali-bongo/

58   https://www.vice.com/en_in/article/jgedjb/the-first-use-
       of-deepfakes-in-indian-election-by-bjp

59   https://www.synthesia.io/post/david-beckham

Notes to 5 AI and the world of work   pages 109–126

60   https://dl.acm.org/doi/pdf/10.1145/3313831.3376718

61   https://finale.seas.harvard.edu/files/finale/files/integrating_
       ai_recommendations_into_the_pharmacologic_management_
       of_major_depressive_disorder.pdf

62   https://www.statnews.com/2018/07/25/ibm-watson-
       recommended-unsafe-incorrect-treatments/

63   https://www.wsj.com/articles/walmart-shelves-plan-to-
       have-robots-scan-shelves-11604345341?st=8ibb9pvqtng6zrt
       &reflink=article_gmail_share

64   https://web-assets.bcg.com/fl/79/cf4f7dce459686cfee20
      edf3117c/mit-bcg-expanding-ai-impact-with-organizational-
      learning-oct-2020.pdf

Notes to 6 Weaponising AI   pages 127–139

65   https://cset.georgetown.edu/wp-content/uploads/Chinese-
      Public-AI-RD-Spending-Provisional-Findings-1.pdf

66   https://medium.com/ai2-blog/china-to-overtake-us-in-ai-
      research-8b6b1fe30595

67   https://arxiv.org/pdf/1707.08945.pdf

68   https://arxiv.org/pdf/1707.07397.pdf

69   https://openai.com/blog/adversarial-example-research/

70   https://arxiv.org/pdf/1312.6199.pdf

71   https://arxiv.org/pdf/1610.08401v1.pdf

72   https://www.cs.cmu.edu/~sbhagava/papers/face-rec-ccs16
      .pdf

73   http://sandlab.cs.uchicago.edu/fawkes/

74   https://arxiv.org/pdf/1312.6199.pdf

75   https://www.wired.co.uk/article/artificial-intelligence-
      hacking-machine-learning-adversarial

76   https://www.vice.com/en/article/pan9wn/hackers-
      hijacked-asus-software-updates-to-install-backdoors-on-
      thousands-of-computers

77   https://pages.nist.gov/trojai/docs/about.html

Notes to 7 Making AI accountable   pages 141–160

78   http://cdn.aiindex.org/2018/AI%20Index%202018%20
      Annual%20Report.pdf

79   https://www.nesta.org.uk/report/gender-diversity-ai/

80   https://reports.weforum.org/global-gender-gap-report-
      2018/assessing-gender-gaps-in-artificial-intelligence/
      #view/fn-22

81   https://ainowinstitute.org/discriminatingsystems.pdf

82   https://ainowinstitute.org/discriminatingsystems.pdf

83   https://arxiv.org/abs/2007.04068

84   https://www.bbc.co.uk/news/technology-55281862

85   https://googlewalkout.medium.com/standing-with-
      dr-timnit-gebru-isupporttimnit-believeblackwomen-
      6dadc300d382

86   https://www.theverge.com/2020/12/9/22165983/google-
       ceo-sundar-pichai-apology-timnit-gebru-exit

87   http://proceedings.mlr.press/v81/buolamwini18a/
       buolamwini18a.pdf

88   https://www.media.mit.edu/publications/actionable-
       auditing-investigating-the-impact-of-publicly-naming-
       biased-performance-results-of-commercial-ai-products/

89   https://algoritmeregister.amsterdam.nl/en/automated-
       parking-control/

90   https://www.wired.co.uk/article/police-violence-
       prediction-ndas

91   https://data.govt.nz/use-data/data-ethics/government-
       algorithm-transparency-and-accountability/algorithm-
       charter

92   https://www.youtube.com/watch?v=DrizMdMq6Mg

Notes to 8 The future of AI   pages 161–167

93   https://www.cnbc.com/2017/07/17/elon-musk-robots-will-
       be-able-to-do-everything-better-than-us.html

94   https://futureoflife.org/ai-open-letter/?cn-reloaded=1

95   https://arxiv.org/pdf/1805.01109.pdf

96   https://arxiv.org/pdf/1705.08807.pdf

97   https://www.theverge.com/2018/11/27/18114362/ai-artificial-general-intelligence-when-achieved-martin-ford-book

98   https://www.quantamagazine.org/google-and-ibm-clash-over-quantum-supremacy-claim-20191023

Index

INDEX

INDEX

INDEX